Testing Python

Testing Python®

APPLYING UNIT TESTING, TDD, BDD, AND ACCEPTANCE TESTING

David Sale

WILEY

This edition first published 2014

© 2014 David Sale

Registered office

John Wiley & Sons Ltd, The Atrium, Southern Gate, Chichester, West Sussex, PO19 8SQ, United Kingdom

For details of our global editorial offices, for customer services and for information about how to apply for permission to reuse the copyright material in this book please see our website at www.wiley.com.

The right of the author to be identified as the author of this work has been asserted in accordance with the Copyright, Designs and Patents Act 1988.

Wiley also publishes its books in a variety of electronic formats. Some content that appears in print may not be available in electronic books.

Designations used by companies to distinguish their products are often claimed as trademarks. All brand names and product names used in this book are trade names, service marks, trademarks or registered trademarks of their respective owners. The publisher is not associated with any product or vendor mentioned in this book. This publication is designed to provide accurate and authoritative information in regard to the subject matter covered. It is sold on the understanding that the publisher is not engaged in rendering professional services. If professional advice or other expert assistance is required, the services of a competent professional should be sought.

Trademarks: Wiley and the Wiley logo are trademarks or registered trademarks of John Wiley & Sons, Inc. and/or its affiliates in the United States and/or other countries, and may not be used without written permission. Python is a registered trademark of the Python Software Foundation. All other trademarks are the property of their respective owners. John Wiley & Sons, Ltd. is not associated with any product or vendor mentioned in the book.

A catalogue record for this book is available from the British Library.

ISBN 978-1-118-90122-9 (paperback); ISBN 978-1-118-90124-3 (ePub); 978-1-118-90125-0 (ePDF)

Set in 10/12.5 ChaparralPro-Light by TCS/SPS

Printed in the USA by Bind-Rite

Publisher's Acknowledgements

Some of the people who helped bring this book to market include the following:

Editorial and Production

VP Consumer and Technology Publishing Director:
Michelle Leete

Associate Director–Book Content Management:
Martin Tribe

Associate Publisher:
Chris Webb

Executive Commissioning Editor:
Craig Smith

Project Editor:
Sydney Argenta

Copy Editor:
Debbye Butler

Technical Editors:
Jeff Yonker, Alex Bradbury,
Andrew Robinson, and Harry Percival

Editorial Manager:
Rev Mengle

Senior Project Editor:
Sara Shlaer

Editorial Assistant:
Claire Johnson

Marketing

Marketing Manager:
Lorna Mein

Assistant Marketing Manager:
Dave Allen

About the Author

DAVID SALE is a Software Developer currently working at British Sky Broadcasting (BSkyB) in London, UK as of 2014. He obtained a degree in Computing at the University of Leeds. Whilst studying Computing, Python was taught as the main programming language of the course. This is very different to many other University's where languages such as Java are taught initially.

This is where David's interest in Python first began and he has looked to further his knowledge in what has become his core programming language.

Following University, David joined BSkyB in September 2011, as part of the Software Engineering Academy graduate scheme. The scheme proved to be an excellent platform for David to launch his career in software development.

Notably, David has worked on a RESTful Python application that models BSkyB's products and offers, applies complex pricing rules and business logic, whilst delivering a completely data driven approach to the problem. David has also worked on a project using a Hypermedia approach to sharing data across the application stack to deliver an innovative solution delivering sales to existing customers of BSkyB.

David quickly began making his presence known in the Python Community, having written web articles on various Python topics. David has also given talks on Behaviour Driven Development and Agile Development at the EuroPython conference, which was held in Florence, Italy in 2012 and 2013 respectively, with videos of the talks available on YouTube.

David follows Agile Development principles whilst working at BSkyB, with pair programming and Test/Behaviour Driven Development a must. From this focus on testing from such an early point in his career, he has picked up many tips and techniques in Python testing which allows development of quality software, which the business has up most confidence in. It is hoped the tips and advice in this book allow you to learn and improve your daily testing skills in Python.

You can find more on David's current and previous projects at: www.dsale.co.uk.

Acknowledgments

First and foremost I would like to thank Craig Smith, Executive Commissioning Editor at Wiley for approaching me with the opportunity to write this book and giving me the confidence in my writing to go for this project; Sydney Jones Argenta, Project Editor, for editing the book so diligently and keeping me up to date throughout the project; Jeff Younker, Alex Bradbury, Andrew Robinson, and Harry Percival Technical Editors for ensuring my code was up to the standard expected by the community and the best it could be.

Secondly, I'd like to give my gratitude to my employer British Sky Broadcasting (Sky). I joined Sky through their Software Engineering Academy graduate scheme and have since progressed to a Software Developer. Without their investment in me, I would not have learned some of the skills and advice that I can now share in this book. They also happily granted me permission to work on this book and helped me find the time to deliver the project alongside my work commitments. Please visit http://workforsky.com if you are interested in joining the team or www.skygraduates.com for more on graduate schemes at Sky.

I'd like to thank my partner Katherine Sweeney, for being so patient in supporting me whilst working on this book. Without her love and support, I would never have dreamed to deliver a project like this and she constantly reminds me to believe in myself. This book is an achievement for us together and I am thankful to have her by my side.

Finally, I would like to thank my brothers Stefan and Matthew Sale for always supporting me in my endeavours but in particular my parents, Ronald and Jennifer Sale. From an early age I have always been taught to work hard and reach for your goals. This book is testament to those words and without the drive to achieve that they have passed on to me; I could never have seen such a big project through. This book is for them and all the people who have supported me in my career as a Software Developer.

Contents

CHAPTER 4
Writing Testable Documentation **55**

CHAPTER 5
Driving Your Development with Tests **67**

Introduction

IF YOU HAVE picked up this book, you clearly have some interest in the world of Python. Perhaps you have just started to learn the language. Maybe you have some Python experience and are looking to learn more about the world of testing. You also could have many years of Python under your belt and want to refresh your testing skills. Whatever your reasons, you will pick up some new skills.

The book covers testing right through from its history looking at how testing in Python has evolved over the years to where it is now, and a brief look at the different practices used. You also look at reasons for testing and why it can be so important in both large enterprise class projects and in small personal projects.

The book lets you get your hands dirty with the basic building blocks in testing, which are unit tests. Here you will be taken through what a unit test is, the basic syntax, and examples of a simple unit test. Then, you take a comprehensive look at the methods available to use in unit testing and the various tools available to help in running and debugging your tests. Wrapping up the unit test section, you look into the pivotal use of mocks and patching, which allow you to isolate the code you are interested in testing (your "units"), and simulate responses from other parts of the system or libraries.

Testing in your documentation is one of the more interesting parts of Python testing. This section shows you how to effectively embed unit tests in your doc strings and have them run as tests. Here you look at why this might be useful to you and go through some examples on writing these yourself.

Your attention then turns to the more recent hot topic of test driven development (TDD), a practice which if followed correctly can ensure you deliver great code that does exactly what you need it to the first time. The TDD section introduces the concepts and ethos of the practice and covers steps required to adopt it. I provide great use cases using TDD in pair programming and show how you can make the development process more fun. Wrapping up the section are examples of test-driving the creation of a part of a real application that you can try yourself.

One of the more recent aspects of testing and something the development community as a whole has moved toward is the concept of behavior driven development (BDD) and acceptance testing. This builds on the TDD approach, helping you to construct tests that ensure features of your application meet the acceptance criteria of your stakeholders. Put another way, BDD ensures that you have a testable way of proving the different parts of your application work together to deliver the behavior that you want. BDD and acceptance testing are fantastic ways of testing and providing documentation supporting your application as the tests are being written—all in a human readable feature file, with code executing underneath. If you have never written this style of test, you'll certainly want to give Chapters 6 and 7 a read.

A key aspect of an application's lifestyle is testing how it will perform under real-life conditions. Your application might be really responsive when running locally on your development machine, but what if your application is going to be accessed by hundreds or thousands of people a minute? Will it respond to requests quickly enough? Will the user experience be affected at all? Performance testing ensures you find the answers to these questions before your customers do, and that can only be a good thing!

The book also covers keeping your code in check. In the development cycle, you write a lot of code and in the majority of cases this code needs to be read by someone other than you. This means effective, actionable standards need to be applied across the Python community. This is where PEP-8 came in and tools have evolved around this to help maintain the standards. You look at effective ways to use tools such as PyLint and code coverage to ensure your code is maintainable, and your tests cover the parts of your application that matter.

A key feature of many teams is having some form of build process. If you have never heard of Jenkins or continuous integration, this section will guide you through why having a build is so important. Continuous integration or "CI" (Jenkins being a tool that helps you manage and run CI) is essentially a process where upon check in of your code to some source control system, that code is put through a series of repeatable tests, profiling, and other metrics to give the team a status of their code at any time. Should tests fail or your code start responding more slowly, then the team is made aware of it quickly and can deal with any issue during the development process. Implementing the build process can make your development processes easier, making use of automation for the things you need to do every day. You wrap up with incorporating useful plug-ins, which can keep track of those PyLint issues and code coverage.

After applying all these techniques and processes to your application, you should then be nearing release of your product! This is where you take a look into smoke testing (a type of testing which shows different components of an application are working together correctly) and how you can have tests in place to ensure every time you release, the wider application stack can work as it did previously with your new code. By taking a look at some of this book's examples and ideas, you should be able to get a smoke-testing suite in place to give you confidence every time you release.

Hopefully, this has whetted your appetite for more on all these Python testing topics. Whether a novice or a Python expert, you should gain something from this book that can help you make your testing better, give you more confidence in your code, and get your whole team involved and engaged in delivering quality every time.

Chapter 1
A History of Testing

THE IDEA OF testing is one that has evolved over many years in the development community. Developers used to have much less focus on testing up front and just wrote code and dealt with any problems that arose by quickly writing fixes after a testing period at the end of a project. That isn't to say that there weren't developers out there who were writing code that was trouble free when out in the wild, but on the whole, writing code without tests in general is going to lead to problems down the line. There were also cases where testing was a priority, such as code that could cause destruction or the possibility of a person dying. In such circumstances there would be rigorous testing, but this was very much the exception rather than the rule.

The first real change in ideology came with improvements in technology and the resulting development pressures that came with it. When computers were slower, code modification cycles took much longer. Even a simple program could take tens of minutes to build, and large projects could take hours. This resulted in a batch development process where people spent a great deal of time pouring over code, figuring out issues, and then making sets of changes. The amount of time spent verifying changes to the code was comparatively small compared with the cycle time.

As computers became faster, compilation times shrank and development cycle times correspondingly shrank. It became feasible to make small changes to code, quickly build the product, and then verify the results of those few changes. This meant that code was written and tests covered that code to ensure it behaved as expected. Also, as computer systems became more powerful, the complexity of software increased. Even a simple program these days often has both a client and server component running on different systems (such as a browser and web server). Operating systems offer a bewildering variety of services to a program. Choreographing these interactions requires managing complexity in a systematic way. Features of Python such as loose typing impose additional verification demands on developers, as errors in coding cannot be caught at a compilation stage. Similarly, because Python has no demands on the type of objects it is manipulating, you can end up with strange behavior if you have not handled all cases correctly.

Testing forces developers to think about the code that they are writing and consider all sorts of different scenarios and the outcomes rather than focusing on the happy path scenario that takes into account only how the code should be used. When combined with a test driven development approach (TDD; see Chapter 5), this ideology ensured that testing was baked in to the development process and not a tedious afterthought. One of the worst traps a developer can fall into is writing a bunch of code and then going back and testing it all at the end. Not only is this approach more time consuming and often rushed, but it also means revisiting code that isn't fresh in the mind like it was at the time of writing. When you revisit the method to write a test, the context and thought process at the time of writing is often lost to you.

Similarly, the change from the waterfall development processes to agile has brought a huge focus on testing while developing rather than treating testing as an afterthought, as I describe previously. Agile development advocates that teams include dedicated quality assurance (QA) personnel, whose sole focus is to write tests and maintain a solid test suite around the application. This allows someone who hasn't written the code to look at it from a fresh angle and perhaps spot weaknesses or bugs in the code before those glitches reach the customer.

Following on from TDD, agile development also spawned the concept of behavior driven development (BDD; see Chapter 6). This method takes unit testing one step further and looks to test the application's behavior in terms of functionality being delivered. BDD is also known as an acceptance test and generally comes in the form of a human readable feature file, which describes the functionality and then maps to step files, which execute the test code underneath. The huge benefit of this approach is that non-technical team members, such as a scrum master (person responsible for removing impediments that arise in a team and assists in organizational matters) or product owner (person wanting the deliverable and setting the requirements for the project), can write feature files, and then the developer or QA can implement the code underneath. With this setup in place, you basically have testable documentation for your system that anyone on the team can understand. This approach also allows you to create a failing acceptance test that you develop your code to pass, ensuring that you deliver the feature you have set out to create. Unit testing alone does not produce such reliable results. It is the combination of the two testing practices that ensures you can deliver quality software and be confident when it goes live.

Clearly, the mindset of developers has changed over the years from not just writing code but to ensuring that their code is tested from all angles. From unit testing to acceptance testing, Python developers have implemented libraries and tools to help Python developers follow these changes to the development process. This book covers their implementation and usage so that you too can get up to speed on the latest testing tools and techniques to ensure you are not left stuck in the past of testing history.

You Do Test, Don't You?

A huge shift has occurred in recent years of software development toward testing and ensuring that your application delivers absolute quality. With the advent of social networks and the ever-increasing pressure of media attention, defects in your code could be costly to both you and your reputation or that of any company you may represent. Whether it be security flaws exposing sensitive customer data, defects that allow hackers access to deface your website, or simply a payments page failing to execute orders, errors can cost your business huge sums of money.

Don't think of problems on only the large-scale, either. Without a proper testing suite in place, how do you know you have delivered the functionality you set out to deliver at the beginning of writing code? Take a simple data submission form. You have coded the fields to accept a name, address, and e-mail, without any testing. You quickly enter the data as expected and your submit works fine. But what if your customers enter something you didn't expect in the fields—for instance, a number in the name field? Does your code handle this? What if you make changes to the code? Are you sure that the program still functions as it should?

You can see some of the problems developers face when writing code of this nature and how testing can give you a repeatable process that ensures you are delivering working software every time. Luckily for you, this shift in mindset to place such importance in testing has spawned numerous, quality testing tools and frameworks to make the process as simple as possible.

You can certainly make great code without tests. In fact, it is highly likely that many software houses put out software without rigorous testing. The key advantage of writing tests, especially as part of the development process, is that testing gives you confidence in your code before it goes live. As a developer, you are often on call to support your applications in the middle of the night. Do you really want that phone call at 3 a.m. because you didn't write tests to cover that edge case? Testing won't stop this from ever happening again, but it will make it a very rare occurrence. You will have good knowledge of the different routes through your system, making it easier to debug the situations where the worst may happen.

Fundamentals and Best Practices

Before getting stuck in the process of writing tests, it is a good idea to take some time to get your machine in order and up to date with the tools you will need to proceed. First, ensure you have the correct version of Python installed. Then, getting set up with some of the basic tools Python developers use on a daily basis will mean you can easily follow the rest of this book and install libraries of code and keep your changes in check using source control. This section is essentially a prerequisite to the rest of the book, and it is recommended you follow the instructions carefully to get your machine in shape for the examples that will follow later.

Python Installation

Of course, this book assumes that you already have some background in Python programming, even at the most basic level. That said, for completeness it is worth mentioning how to get Python on your system and what version this book uses.

The book focuses on the Python 2.7 release, which is used quite widely in the Python community. It is the last version that was released prior to the backward-incompatible release of 3.0 and beyond. The vast majority of code will likely work with Python 3.0 and the official documentation will help with any problems that may arise.

Linux

Most Linux distributions come with some version of Python installed. Most notably, recent Ubuntu releases generally come with version 2.7.*x* preinstalled. If for some reason you find you don't have Python, or perhaps you have an older version and want to upgrade, you usually install using your distributions package manager. Should Python not be available in this form, then you can visit `www.python.org` to download the source and compile it yourself. Instructions should be included on the website.

Mac

Like Linux, Apple chose to ship a version of Python with every version of OS X. At the time of writing, Mavericks had just been released in October 2013; this version included Python 2.7.5 by default. Therefore, if you are following this book and working on a Mac, then you should be all set. If you find you need to get Python on your machine for some reason, then you could install a package manager for Mac. This not only will help with the install of Python itself, but will also come in handy for any other dependencies your system may need. Two popular package managers for Mac are available: MacPorts and Homebrew. I prefer the latter because its packages seem to be better maintained and more up to date than those for MacPorts. Homebrew is also a more lightweight installation, and the install scripts are written in Ruby, which means it's easy to write some brews yourself. You can find information on the two package managers here:

- MacPorts at `http://macports.com`
- Homebrew at `http://brew.sh`

Windows

Windows is considered out of scope in this book. Having had little to no experience working with Python on a Windows machine, I am not in the best place to offer advice. However, that does not mean the code and advice in this book are not of use to a Windows user.

Plenty of guides on the web can help a Windows user get set up with Python, at which point you can easily run the tests and code that this book offers. Some good Python Windows resources are

- Official Python website: `http://www.python.org/downloads/windows/`
- Python documentation: `http://docs.python.org/2/using/windows.html`

Pip

The new standard package manager for Python, Pip allows you to install any of numerous Python packages from the PyPi repository. For example, you may want to write a web application in which case a popular web framework such as Django or Flask could be installed. First find out if you have Python. If so, you also should have Pip. If you don't, you should at least have `easy_install`, the package manager that Pip has superseded. To get Pip in this scenario, simply try:

```
$ easy_install pip
```

You should then have Pip and be able to install packages, like so:

```
$ pip install flask
```

More on `easy_install` and Pip can be found at `http://www.pip-installer.org`.

Virtualenv

If you have been working on any Python projects without using Virtualenv, you are certainly missing out. Virtualenv helps to give you a clean Python environment for every project you work on. With all projects, you generally end up installing at least a few packages. If you use your system Python installation for every project, then you can end up installing many packages and possibly needing different versions of the same package for different projects. You could remove and install the package each time you worked on the project, but Virtualenv removes this headache and keeps your projects separate.

You need to install two packages to use Virtualenv effectively: the Virtualenv package itself, which provides the functionality already described, and Virtualenvwrapper, which is optional but highly recommended. The wrapper basically provides handy command line utilities for creating, deleting, and working with Virtualenvs. For instance, with the wrapper installed you can create a Virtualenv, like so:

```
$ mkvirtualenv myenv
(myenv) $
```

After you create the Virtualenv, it activates automatically. Virtualenv informs you which version you are using by including the Virtualenv name at the start of your command prompt. Another nicety of the wrapper is that you can write your own command hooks to perform actions after, say, activating a Virtualenv. For example, I have set mine up to change into the project directory of the Virtualenv I am activating. I won't go into any more detail on Virtualenv now, but I highly recommend you install it on your machine. You can find all the details here:

- **Virtualenv:** `http://www.virtualenv.org/en/latest/`

- **Virtualenvwrapper:** `https://pypi.python.org/pypi/virtualenvwrapper`

Source Control (SVN, Git)

Version control is vital when working on a project—whether alone or with many developers. Your software will evolve naturally as you work on it, but what if you want to go back to changes made a few days earlier? You may want to try an idea out but need an easy way to revert to the prior working state should your current idea not work. How do you manage multiple developers working on the same code base and but still keep code changes in check? Source control gives you the power to manage all these problems easily, with great tools and integration with things like your favorite IDE. Source control also serves as the integration point for many other processes, such as continuous integration, code review systems, code quality and coverage reporting and release and deployment among others. Therefore it is clear that having a solid, well understood and maintainable source control system in place is crucial and forms a clear backbone to your code base's organization.

The two most commonly used source control systems are Subversion (SVN) and Git. SVN is the older of the two and works based on a single repository model. This means you check out an SVN repository of the code, do your work, and commit the changes back to the repository on the server.

Git, however, flips this model, where you clone a Git repository from the server. You then do some work and commit to your local copy of the repository. You can do as many local commits as you like, before pulling changes from the repository on the server, fixing any conflicts of code, and then pushing their changes to the server to be pulled by other developers. Git is known as a distributed source control for this reason. The main benefits of Git are

- **Local commits:** You can check in without an Internet connection.

- **Branches:** Easily create and switch branches to work on ideas or features away from the main "master" branch.

- **Merge:** Move branches back into the master. Rebase option to replay commits one by one rather than whole changes in one go a la SVN.

- **Git SVN:** Easily convert SVN repository to Git with built-in tools.

The main disadvantage to using Git is the lack of a central source of truth for your project. Because Git allows so much flexibility and freedom with its distributed repository architecture, without careful management you can end up with a confusing project structure and merge issues. With SVN having only the one central repository it makes it simpler for developers to keep their code on their machine up to date and in sync with the rest of the checked in code.

Git is becoming the standard for version control, with the added benefits of the distributed model suiting the workflows of many developers and its handling of merging code much better than SVN.

- **Git:** http://git-scm.com

- **Pro Git (Free eBook on Git):** http://git-scm.com/book

- **Try Git (Free online tutorial):** http://try.github.com/

- **SVN:** http://subversion.apache.org

- **Version Control with SVN (Free eBook):** http://svnbook.red-bean.com/

Interactive Development Environment (IDE)

Using a good IDE can be advantageous. Getting comfortable and familiar with an IDE is much like a car mechanic knowing every tool in his garage. An IDE doesn't make you a good programmer, but knowing how and when to use the right tools can make your life a lot easier. You can usually find a couple of stand-out IDEs for each language, and the development communities have their favorites. Two of my favorites for Python are PyCharm and the more all-encompassing IntelliJ, which handles many programming languages. IntelliJ and PyCharm are essentially the same product provided by Jetbrains, with PyCharm focused only on Python development and IntelliJ utilizing a Python plugin to provide the entire feature set of PyCharm alongside other language support. Both are regularly maintained, with new features releases and bug fixes every couple of months. The IDE is also well designed with support for many popular libraries and frameworks, such as Flask and Django web frameworks, and test support for running tests in the IDE itself instead of the command line and also Virtualenv's discussed earlier.

You also get the usual IDE features of code completion, syntax highlighting, and powerful searching, which is great when working with larger code bases. Both IDEs also offer expansion for many different types of tools you may want to interact with through the use of plug-ins. For example, if you write bash scripts to use with your code, you can install the bash plug-in and write the scripts in the IDE with full syntax highlight and support for adding code items like shebangs. A large repository of plug-ins is available, so should you need some extra functionality, you will likely find it there.

PyCharm, shown in Figure 1-1, is available on a trial, free (with some features unavailable), and full-feature set license basis. Pricing and further information is available at `http://www.jetbrains.com/pycharm/`.

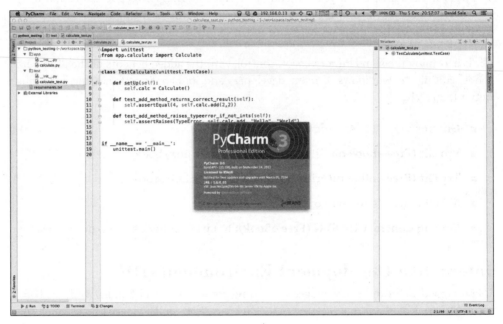

FIGURE 1-1: PyCharm interface. This excellent Python IDE helps you develop great Python code.

Summary

This introductory chapter provided a brief description of whom this book is for. By now, you should have a feel for the concepts and topics that are conveyed in subsequent chapters. You were introduced to the subject of testing and given a brief background in the history of testing. You were shown how it has evolved from merely an afterthought of the product to a process, which in many cases is now baked in to the development.

"You do test, don't you?" poses a great question to many developers and hopefully serves as a reminder throughout your time reading this book and beyond. Testing is an important part of a developer's work and is shown to produce better results, especially in terms of aiming for zero defects in production. You looked into why testing is now such a pivotal process and how it can be beneficial both in a team and lone developer environment.

Finally, the chapter closes by ensuring you have some of the essential Python tooling on your machine, be it Linux, Mac, or Windows. By getting these fundamentals ready, you will be set to take on the examples and ideas in this book and it should also help you in your next projects and beyond.

Chapter 2
Writing Unit Tests

AN APPLICATION IS one of the great examples of the whole being greater than the sum of its parts. As a whole, the application potentially delivers a huge amount of value. Its component parts perform specific functions, which can be useful on their own but deliver more when combined. That said, it is clear that if any of the smaller parts of the application do not function as expected, the application as a whole is flawed or fails completely. This is where unit testing comes in.

In this chapter you learn all about the fundamental testing practice of unit tests. I will cover exactly what a unit test is, how to write one and provide you examples that assist your learning. There is also a comprehensive breakdown of some of the most widely used unit test methods, which you can refer to as a guide when writing any unit tests yourself. This chapter also seeks to convey some of the standards that Python developers expect when they read over unit tests and shows you how you can put them into practice so they become second nature. Finally, this chapter rounds off with some more advanced techniques in unit testing to give you an insight into the further usages and implementations of unit tests.

What Is Unit Testing?

In unit testing, you look to cover the application's functionality at its most basic level. Test each individual unit of code, typically a method, in isolation to see if given certain conditions it responds in the expected way (see Figure 2-1). Breaking testing down to this level gives you confidence that each part of the application will behave as expected and enables you to cover edge cases where the unexpected happens and deal with them accordingly.

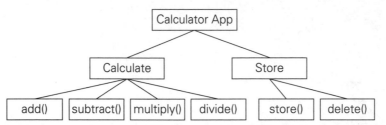

FIGURE 2-1: Example application structure showing the classes and methods. The methods are the "units" you will test.

In the preceding example, the methods highlighted are the individual units of this application that you need to test. If you know that each of the `calculate` class's methods work as expected, you can be confident that the calculate feature of your application has been delivered to your expectations.

For instance, you may wish to test whether the result of calling the method with two numbers actually adds them together to produce the correct sum. Breaking your code down into these units makes the testing process easier. When dealing with a small unit of an application, you have a clear understanding of its responsibilities and the things that can go wrong with the specific piece of code, thus enabling you to cover the unit with the appropriate tests.

Furthermore, when testing in this manner it usually becomes obvious if you have broken down the code into a good-sized unit. If you have to write many different tests to cover all the different possibilities that the method can go through, your method may be too large and you should consider refactoring it into two or more methods with fine-grained responsibilities. Conversely, there may be cases where your method is too simple and could be combined with some other functionality to create a more useful method. As a programmer with experience, you should start to get a feel for a good-sized method. Ten lines is often a good rule of thumb to follow. There are, of course, plenty of cases where you need more or less than this arbitrary number of lines, and as a programmer your common sense should guide you to provide the most readable code.

The tests that you write are a story that explains your code. What would you want to read or see when first reading through the code and trying to understand what it does? Clear, concise naming conventions of variables, class names, filenames, and tests can all help to make your code clear and easy to maintain for other people.

Testing and, in particular, test driven development (TDD; see Chapter 5), can really help to achieve these goals. TDD forces you to think about your code, and in this moment of careful consideration you can take into account the needs of the application, the design of the code, and how other programmers will interpret your intentions. Use testing to your advantage to make your code cleaner and more efficient. With a good test suite in place, refactoring is easy because you know when you change your code you haven't broken any previous behavior. The tests take the guesswork out of your development process and you can deliver great applications, knowing you have delivered something robust and reliable.

What Should You Test?

A question that many developers ask especially when first starting out is, what should I test? This is an interesting question and also a fair one, as the applications that are being built now are often vast with many complexities. However, unit testing makes the task easier as the whole idea is to focus on the smallest units of code rather than thinking about how to test the large application you are putting together as a whole. Before you write any code you give thought to the kind of tests you will be writing to check the methods will work as expected. As you write more and more unit tests you will gain experience in what works well and what perhaps causes you issues later down the line. For example, a frequent mistake of inexperienced developers is writing very brittle test suites. This means that as code evolves the tests break for reasons other than the functionality changing. The tests are often checking elements of the code or data to too fine a granularity, meaning that as data changes (and not your functionality, which is what you are really testing), the tests fail and you need to go and fix it. Making your tests as flexible as possible while still testing your functionality is the best way to defend against this brittleness.

Another reason to test comes from the process of finding bugs whether in a production environment, the test environment, or while testing your application locally. Whenever you find a bug that affects your application that requires a code change to fix, you should write a test to cover that scenario. By doing this, you ensure that you have covered the defect that caused the problem and with test in place the bug should not reoccur in the future. By adding this layer of defense every time you find a bug (hopefully, not very often) you ensure that your code is more robust in the future as more functionality is added.

Writing Your First Unit Test

By now, you are probably eager to start writing your first unit test. Perhaps you have written tests before but are looking for a refresher in how to write good, concise unit tests. Whatever your Python or testing background, let's start at the beginning with some simple tests for a straightforward application. The examples first show you how to structure your test into a class with the correct naming conventions. Further on in the chapter, you are simply shown snippets of test methods, which you are expected to use with a proper test class.

One of the classic examples for demonstrating unit testing is a small calculator program. Python actually includes a lot of basic math functionality in the standard library. But what if you wrapped that into a simple-to-use command line application that could perform some simple calculations? This first scenario demonstrates how to implement the calculate class of the application example from earlier. Start with the add method, which looks something like this.

```
class Calculate(object):
    def add(self, x, y):
        return x + y

if __name__ == '__main__':
    calc = Calculate()
    result = calc.add(2, 2)
    print result
```

Clearly, this is a very simple class that is just making use of Python's built-in math function for adding and making it into a method you can call in your code. Save this code to a file named calculate.py, then execute this and see the result, like so.

```
$ python calculate.py
4
```

Checking Values with the assertEquals Method

You have some working code, so why not write the tests to prove it and look into what could go wrong if the code is used in ways you didn't foresee? Try writing a test that checks to see that if you pass in the two numbers as 2, then you get the result as 4. Using the standard Python library, you can import the unittest package. This provides useful methods to make different kinds of assertions (for instance, checking whether something meets some condition) on your method. One of those assertions you can use is the assertEqual method. This method allows you to pass in two values and check whether they are equal.

Create a test file called calculate_test.py, following the standard naming conventions of using the class name under test and appending with _test.

```
import unittest
from app.calculate import Calculate


class TestCalculate(unittest.TestCase):
    def setUp(self):
        self.calc = Calculate()
```

```
    def test_add_method_returns_correct_result(self):
        self.assertEqual(4, self.calc.add(2,2))


if __name__ == '__main__':
    unittest.main()
```

A line-by-line examination shows that this example first imports the functionality you need from Python's `unittest` module. You are also importing your own class, `Calculate`, so that you can test its methods. You do this in the `setUp` method, which is executed before each test, so that you need define your instance only once and have it created before each test. Then you can write your test and again the standard is to append your test name with `append_test` and explain what the test is doing briefly in the rest of the name. Here you are checking if the `add` method returns the correct result. To do this, you make use of the `assertEqual` method provided by the imported `unittest` module. This checks if the first argument is equal to the second. In this example, you are checking whether 4 is equal to the result of calling your `add` method on 2 and 2. In this case, the test passes as your code works and displays the following result in the terminal.

```
$ python test/calculate_test.py
.
----------------------------------------------------------------------
---
Ran 1 test in 0.000s
OK
```

This shows you that your test ran okay, and you ran only the one test. What if things go wrong? You can simulate that by breaking the test. Change `test_add_method_returns_correct_result` to assert that 2 add 3 equals 4, then you should see a failing test.

```
import unittest
from app.calculate import Calculate


class TestCalculate(unittest.TestCase):
    ...
    def test_add_method_returns_correct_result(self):
        self.assertEqual(4, self.calc.add(2,3))
    ...

$ python test/calculate_test.py
F
======================================================================
===
```

```
FAIL: test_add_method_returns_correct_result
  (__main__.TestCalculate)
----------------------------------------------------------------
 - - -
Traceback (most recent call last):
  File
  "/Users/user/workspace/python_testing/test/calculate_test.py",
  line 12, in test_add_method_returns_correct_result
    self.assertEqual(4, self.calc.add(2,3))
AssertionError: 4 != 5
----------------------------------------------------------------
 - - -
Ran 1 test in 0.000s
FAILED (failures=1)
```

You can see that the `unittest` module provides great feedback as to what went wrong and where. You can easily go back and fix the test. Of course, a real failure would usually be caused by your code not meeting your expectation and producing the wrong result. In that case, you would need to go in and fix your code. There you have it. You've written your first, simple unit test.

Checking Exception Handling with assertRaises

You have considered what happens in the normal use cases of your method and what happens if it returns the wrong answer. What about if you passed in something the method doesn't expect? You usually would find in such cases an exception to be raised. The `assert Raises` method, also found in the `unittest` package, provides you with a means to check that a method raises an exception under certain circumstances.

Take a look at your Calculator example again. The `add` method would seem to work with only numbers. What if you pass in two strings like `"Hello"` and `"World"`? Change the piece of code from calculate_test.py to do that.

```
if __name__ == '__main__':
    calc = Calculate()
    result = calc.add("Hello", "World")
    print result
```

Execute the code and see what you get.

```
$ python calculator.py
HelloWorld
```

Because Python isn't strongly typed, you can pass any type of object to `app/calculate.py`'s `add` method and it will try to combine the objects if it can. Again, if this is functionality you would like in your application, you can write a test for it, as before. If you specifically want to stop this behavior, you could try to check the type and allow only numbers to be added.

```
def add(self, x, y):
    if type(x) == int and type(y) == int:
        return x + y
    else:
        raise TypeError("Invalid type: {} and {}".format(type(x),
            type(y)))
```

This works fine when passing in two integers, but what if you try to add a number and a string? You will likely run into problems there.

```
class TestCalculate(unittest.TestCase):

    def setUp(self):
        self.calc = Calculate()

    def test_add_method_returns_correct_result(self):
        self.assertEqual("HelloWorld", self.calc.add("Hello",
"World"))
```

```
$ python test/calculate_test.py
E
================================================================
ERROR: test_add_method_returns_correct_result
 (__main__.TestCalculate)
----------------------------------------------------------------
------
Traceback (most recent call last):
  File
"/Users/username/workspace/python_testing/test/calculate_test.py"
, line 11, in test_add_method_returns_correct_result
    self.assertEqual(4, self.calc.add("Hello", "World"))
  File "/Users/username/workspace/python_testing/app/calculate.py",
line 10, in add
    raise TypeError("Invalid type: {} and {}".format(type(x),
type(y)))
TypeError: Invalid type: <type 'str'> and <type 'str'>
----------------------------------------------------------------
---
Ran 1 test in 0.000s
```

As expected, your code raises the error with the message you have defined to indicate what the problem is. As the types of the object passed in are strings, they don't meet the if statement's criteria and so it raises a `TypeError`.

Now that you have defined this as wanted behavior from your method, you can write a test to cover this. Write new test that checks that the `TypeError` is raised when you do pass in strings. For this type of test, you make use of the `assertRaises` method that `unittest` provides. The unit test method `assertRaises` takes three arguments. The first is the type of exception you expect to be raised, in this case `TypeError`. The second is the method under test, in this case `self.calc.add` that you expect to raise this exception. The final value passed in is the argument to the method under test, in this case the string `"Hello"`.

```
def test_add_method_raises_typeerror_if_not_ints(self):
    self.assertRaises(TypeError, self.calc.add, "Hello",
        "World")
$ python test/calculate_test.py
..
-------------------------------------------------------------
------
Ran 2 tests in 0.000s
OK
```

Following the PEP-8 Standard

As I have been introducing you to unit testing in Python, it should be clear that various patterns and standards are followed within the Python community. Some of them are enforced by tools you may wish to use, such as prepending a test name with `test_` to allow runners such as Nose to find tests to execute. Others are merely standards set by Python developers to keep readability and reuse of code high as it is shared between developers. It helps to give Python code a consistent look and feel that experienced developers are familiar with, and if teams adhere to the accepted standards then when developers move to a new Python project, many aspects of the code should feel familiar.

All Python developers code should conform to the standards outlined within the PEP-8 document (available on the Python website at `http://legacy.python.org/dev/peps/pep-0008/`). Guido van Rossum, creator of the Python language, along with Barry Warsaw and Nick Coghlan, writes the style guide. The document is one of the most famous PEPs (Python Enhancement Proposals) and also one of the earliest. PEPs are put forward as suggestions for changes to the language or how to use it. PEP-8 focuses on the styling of code and puts forward some of the fundamental principles when writing Python code and tests, such as:

- **Indents:** Four spaces for each indentation

```
def foo():
    print "Hello, World!"
```

- **Maximum line length:** 80 characters.

- **Blank lines:** Two between import, class, and function definitions. One between method definitions inside a class.

- **Import statements:** Should be one per line.

```
import os
import sys
```

- **Class names:** Should have capitals for the first letter of each word.

```
class MyClass(object):
```

- **Method names:** Should use all lowercase and underscores to separate words.

```
def my_method_example():
```

You should endeavor to maintain these standards and use them throughout the code you write. You will also see them followed throughout this book. You can find the whole PEP-8 document and others at `www.python.org/dev/peps/`. Fortunately, tools have been created to keep your code in check with the standard, such as PyLint. I cover them in detail in Chapter 9.

Unit Test Structure

When structuring your project, you can follow some clear standards to make your application's code more accessible to other Python developers. These simple rules are easy to apply and result in a uniform structure to make it easy to find the test and code files you need.

- Unit tests should be placed under a `test/unit` directory at the top level of your project folder.

- All folders within the application's code should be mirrored by test folders under `test/unit`, which will have the unit tests for each file in them. For example, `app/data` should have a mirrored folder of `test/unit/app/data`.

- All unit test files should mirror the name of the file they are testing, with `_test`as the suffix. For example, `app/data/data_interface.py` should have a test file of `test/unit/app/data/data_interface_test.py`.

To illustrate these rules even more, take a look at one example of how you might structure a Flask project. Flask is the Python web framework package, which you can read more about at `http://flask.pocoo.org`.

```
example_app/
  example_app/
    __init__.py
    static/
    templates/
    app.py
  test/
      __init__.py
    unit/
        __init__.py
      app_test.py
```

The `__init__.py` files indicate that the folder is a Python package so that you can import them into other Python files. For example, in `app_test.py`, you need to import methods from `app.py` so that you can test it.

You are, of course, free to structure your project however you like. This is simply a recommended structure that many developers follow.

Additional Unit Test Examples

By now, you have written your first unit test, been introduced to the multitude of testing methods you have at your disposal, and looked at the standards and structures you should follow when creating your unit tests.

Now take a look at some additional examples of unit tests in action and highlight some key points to note against each one.

Getting Clever with assertRaises

In certain situations, `assertRaises` does not appear to work as expected. For instance, when the exception-causing situation is due to calling a method that does not exist on the object, you get an `AttributeError`. However, when you attempt to test for this in the usual manner, you get the following result:

```
def test_assert_raises(self):
    self.assertRaises(AttributeError, [].get)
```

```
$ python test/example_test.py
E
=====================================================================
===
ERROR: test_assert_raises (__main__.TestExample)
---------------------------------------------------------------
---
Traceback (most recent call last):
  File
  "/Users/username/workspace/python_testing/test/example_test.py",
  line 77, in test_assert_raises
    self.assertRaises(AttributeError, [].get)
AttributeError: 'list' object has no attribute 'get'


---------------------------------------------------------------
---
Ran 19 tests in 0.001s
FAILED (errors=1)
```

Although your expected exception has been raised, the test fails because the exception is not caught by the test method. Fortunately, the `assertRaises` method provides the capability to use it as a context manager. This means you can execute any code you like within the context of `assertRaises`, and if the exception is raised it will be caught and your test will pass as expected.

```
def test_assert_raises(self):
    with self.assertRaises(AttributeError):
        [].get
```

```
$ python test/example_test.py
.
---------------------------------------------------------------
---
Ran 19 tests in 0.001s

OK
```

Making Your Life Easier with setUp

Unit testing often includes a lot of repeated code. You generally need to create instances of classes to be able to use the methods on them in multiple tests. Following good software development practices such as D.R.Y (**D**on't **R**epeat **Y**ourself) and *Clean Code: A Handbook of Agile Software Craftsmanship* by Robert Cecil Martin (Prentice–Hall, 978-0132350884), you should avoid duplicating code and keep tests as succinct as possible.

Following these principles means that changes to your tests are kept to a minimum; a mistake in duplicated code will need to be changed everywhere it was used. It also ensures your tests are easier to debug. If the test is literally executing the code it is designed to test as opposed to multiple lines of setup, then the developer will be able to clearly see the point of failure and aid in getting the problem fixed.

This is where the setUp method comes in. Although oddly named by Python conventions (it perhaps should be set_up or setup), this aspect of unit testing is powerful and minimizes the code you need to write down. Next I use the calculator example with and without the setUp method to illustrate.

Without Setup
```
class TestCalculate(unittest.TestCase):
    def test_add_method_returns_correct_result(self):
      calc = Calculate()
        self.assertEqual(4, calc.add(2,2))

    def test_add_method_raises_typeerror_if_not_ints(self):
        calc = Calculate()
        self.assertRaises(TypeError, calc.add, "Hello", "World")

if __name__ == '__main__':
    unittest.main()
```

With Setup
```
class TestCalculate(unittest.TestCase):

    def setUp(self):
        self.calc = Calculate()

    def test_add_method_returns_correct_result(self):
        self.assertEqual(4, self.calc.add(2,2))

    def test_add_method_raises_typeerror_if_not_ints(self):
        self.assertRaises(TypeError, self.calc.add, "Hello",
  "World")

if __name__ == '__main__':
    unittest.main()
```

Even in this simple test case scenario, the addition of the `setUp` method means you only need to create the instance of `Calculate` once for it to be available to all test cases. Imagine how advantageous it is to be able to create this just once if you needed to test many more scenarios than just these two. Say, for example, you hadn't used the `setUp` but created the `Calculate` class in each test case. Say your class had grown and you now had 15 test cases where this is now created. What if the initializer for `Calculate` changed and you now needed to pass in some new variables to the class? Instead of just one change in the `setUp`, you now need to change 15 lines of code.

It should be noted that even through the use of `setUp`, there is nothing to stop you having some test case which doesn't make use of the objects created in the setup. Perhaps you need to test a slightly different scenario, which requires a different `setUp`. In this case you can just use locally created variables rather than the class level objects the `setUp` method will provide. This is more obvious in cases where you need to mock external libraries or calls. For example, a call to a database might need to be mocked the same way for 90% of your tests, so that would be done in the setup. You may then need to mock it differently to test an error case, which you would do in that test only, ignoring the variables created in the setup.

Useful Methods in Unit Testing

This section provides a quick guide to all the different methods available in the unit test package. For each one, a description of its usage and an example are provided. All methods that take an optional argument, `msg=None`, can be provided a custom message that is displayed on failure.

assertEqual(x, y, msg=None)

This method checks to see whether argument x equals argument y. Under the covers, this method is performing the check using the `==` definition for the objects.

```
def test_assert_equal(self):
    self.assertEqual(1, 1)
```

assertAlmostEqual(x, y, places=None, msg=None, delta=None)

On first glance, this method may seem a little strange but in context becomes useful. The method is basically useful around testing calculations when you want a result to be within a certain amount of places to the expected, or within a certain delta.

```
def test_assert_almost_equal_delta_0_5(self):
    self.assertAlmostEqual(1, 1.2, delta=0.5)

def test_assert_almost_equal_places(self):
    self.assertAlmostEqual(1, 1.00001, places=4)
```

assertRaises(exception, method, arguments, msg=None)

Given a method and set of arguments to that method, does it raise the exception? Arguments must match the signature of the method or syntax error is raised. Arguments are passed as comma-separated lists, not as part of the method call, as shown in the following example:

```
def test_assert_raises(self):
    self.assertRaises(ValueError, int, "a")

def test_assert_raises_alternative(self):
    with self.assertRaises(AttributeError):
        [].get
```

assertDictContainsSubset(expected, actual, msg=None)

Use this method to check whether `actual` contains `expected`. It's useful for checking that part of a dictionary is present in the result, when you are expecting other things to be there also. For example, a large dictionary may be returned and you need to test that only a couple of entries are present.

```
def test_assert_dict_contains_subset(self):
    expected = {'a': 'b'}
    actual = {'a': 'b', 'c': 'd', 'e': 'f'}
    self.assertDictContainsSubset(expected, actual)
```

assertDictEqual(d1, d2, msg=None)

This method asserts that two dictionaries contain exactly the same key value pairs. For this test to pass, the two dictionaries must be exactly the same, but not necessarily in the same order.

```
def test_assert_dict_equal(self):
    expected = {'a': 'b', 'c': 'd'}
    actual = {'c': 'd', 'a': 'b'}
    self.assertDictEqual(expected, actual)
```

assertTrue(expr, msg=None)

Use this method to check the truth value of an expression or result. This method can be useful and has a few interesting caveats. This is because Python's implicit truth behavior, such as numeric values like 0 and 1 have truth-value of `False` and `True`, respectively. Table 2-1 lists some implied truths along with test examples, but more information can be found in the Python documentation.

Table 2-1   **Truth values**

Value	Truth
0	False
1	True
-1	True
""	False
"Hello, World!"	True
None	False

```
def test_assert_true(self):
    self.assertTrue(1)
    self.assertTrue("Hello, World")
```

assertFalse(expr, msg=None)

This method is the inverse of `assertTrue` and is used for checking whether the expression or result under the test is `False`.

```
def test_assert_false(self):
    self.assertFalse(0)
    self.assertFalse("")
```

assertGreater(a, b, msg=None)

This method allows you to check whether one value is greater than the other. It is essentially a helper method that wraps up the use of `assertTrue` on the expression a > b. It displays a helpful message by default when the value is not greater.

```
def test_assert_greater(self):
    self.assertGreater(2, 1)
```

assertGreaterEqual(a, b, msg=None)

You use this method to check whether one value is greater than *or equal to* another value. Essentially, this wrapper is asserting `True` on a >= b. The assertion also gives a nicer message if the expectation is not met.

```
def test_assert_greater_equal(self):
    self.assertGreaterEqual(2, 2)
```

assertIn(member, container, msg=None)

With this method, you can check whether a value is in a container (hashable) such as a list or tuple. This method is useful when you don't care what the other values are, you just wish to check that a certain value(s) is in the container.

```
def test_assert_in(self):
    self.assertIn(1, [1,2,3,4,5])
```

assertIs(expr1, expr2)

Use this method to check that `expr1` and `expr2` are identical. That is to say they are the same object. For example, the python code `[] is []` would return `False`, as the creation of each list is a separate object.

```
def test_assert_is(self):
    self.assertIs("a", "a")
```

assertIsInstance(obj, class, msg=None)

This method asserts that an object is an instance of a specified class. This is useful for checking that the return type of your method is as expected (for instance, if you wish to check that a value is a type of `int`):

```
def test_assert_is_instance(self):
    self.assertIsInstance(1, int)
```

assertNotIsInstance(obj, class, msg=None)

This reverse of `assertIsInstance` provides an easy way to assert that the object is not a type of the class.

```
def test_assert_is_not_instance(self):
    self.assertNotIsInstance(1, str)
```

assertIsNone(obj, msg=None)

Use this to easily check if a value is `None`. This method provides a useful standard message if not `None`.

```
def test_assert_is_none(self):
    self.assertIsNone(None)
```

assertIsNot(expr1, expr2, msg=None)

Using this method, you can check that expr1 is not the same as expr2. This is to say that expr1 is not the same object as expr2.

```
def test_assert_is_not(self):
    self.assertIsNot([], [])
```

assertIsNotNone(obj, msg=None)

This method checks that the value provided is not None. This is useful for checking that your method returns an actual value, rather than nothing.

```
def test_assert_is_not_none(self):
    self.assertIsNotNone(1)
```

assertLess(a, b, msg=None)

This method checks that the value a is less than the value b. This is a wrapper method for assertTrue on a < b.

```
def test_assert_less(self):
    self.assertLess(1, 2)
```

assertLessEqual(a, b, msg=None)

This method checks that the value a is less than or equal to the value b. This is a wrapper method for assertTrue on a <= b.

```
def test_assert_less_equal(self):
    self.assertLessEqual(2, 2)
```

assertItemsEqual(a, b, msg=None)

This assertion is perfect for testing whether two lists are equal. Lists are unordered; therefore, assertEqual on a list can produce intermittent failing tests as the order of the lists may change when running the tests. This can produce a failing test when in fact the two lists have the same contents and are equal.

```
def test_assert_items_equal(self):
    self.assertItemsEqual([1,2,3], [3,1,2])
```

assertRaises(excClass, callableObj, *args, **kwargs, msg=None)

This assertion is used to check that under certain conditions exceptions are raised. You pass in the exception you expect, the callable that will raise the exception and any arguments to that callable. In the earlier example, this pops the first item from an empty list and results in an `IndexError`.

```
def test_assert_raises(self):
    self.assertRaises(IndexError, [].pop, 0)
```

Hopefully, the assertions outlined in this section should be all you need to write any unit tests that exercise your application's functionality. A couple of assertions may be missing from this list. You can find the full `unittest` documentation in the Python documentation at: `http://docs.python.org/2/library/unittest.html`.

Summary

You got down to business in this chapter. You were introduced to the concept of unit testing, breaking down your application into small bite-sized chunks that could be tested in isolation. You wrote your first unit test! By taking a small example application such as a Calculator, you were able to see how to test the individual responsibilities of the class and methods.

You wrote unit tests that make use of the two main assertions in `assertEqual` and `assertRaises` to check happy and unhappy paths through the code. PEP-8 showed Python developers the standards they should adhere to both in code and in tests. By following the guidelines outlined in the PEP-8 document, you can ensure you will write neat, readable Python code that is easily accessible to other Python developers.

A comprehensive guide to the different assertion methods available when unit testing should prove to be a valuable resource to those starting out or brushing up their skills in unit testing. A clear guide to the method names and arguments to be provided makes it easy to get writing unit tests of your own and also maybe discover some methods you weren't aware of.

Finally, I rounded off the chapter with advice on the standard structure and makeup of a typical Python application and its tests. As with PEP-8, following a standard structure ensures it is easier to work on projects with other Python developers, but it is important to do what is best for you and your project should the need arise. Some more advanced unit test cases and improvements completed the chapter to ensure you have everything you need to write good unit tests that exercise your application efficiently.

Chapter 3
Utilizing Unit Test Tools

YOU HAVE STARTED to write your unit tests and feel comfortable running them in the usual manner for executing Python files. However, with testing as much a part of the development process as writing the code itself, it is natural that many tools have surfaced to aid and assist in the running of unit tests as part of the daily development cycle. Whether it be to aid writing the test files themselves or to make running the tests and debugging easier, the tools available help to make you a more productive developer who is better able to build testing into processes such as continuous integration.

This chapter introduces the tools that enable you to work in a better way with your unit testing, giving you useful features such as one-line commands for running your unit tests. You will look at using commonplace tools such as Nosetest and PyTest for running your unit tests and the helpful output and features they provide to make testing easier. I will also cover the integration of these runners with other advanced tools such as coverage reporting and coding style reports. These tools show whether or not lines of code are covered by tests and the lines of code that break coding conventions as outlined in PEP-8. Finally, the chapter finishes by demonstrating the use of mocking and patching within your tests. These strategies allow you to test your application even when making calls to external systems or elements of your application you do not want to call in a test. By mocking and patching in your tests you isolate just the parts of the code you need to test and can set up exactly how you want the external parts of code to respond in the scenario you are testing. Put simply, mocking and patching give you the control to test every type of scenario your code may encounter.

Using Python's Nose

By far, one of the most popular unit test tools in the Python community is the `Nose` package. The Nose developers advertise the package as "Nicer testing for Python" and as an "extension" of the `unittest` package. In this respect, this makes Nose a natural choice for developers who have written unit tests using the `unittest` package, as there is no need to change your tests in any way. What Nose brings is a powerful way to run your tests and have options such as running only the last failed test, ignoring certain tests, tagging, and much more. Nose is also extendable through the use of a variety of plug-ins (a repository of plugins can be found at `https://nose-plugins.jottit.com`). It also gives you the opportunity to create something custom, should your testing situation dictate.

Installing Nose

Before you start to familiarize yourself with Nose's features, you should install the package on your machine. Nose is released with the PyPi repository, and if you followed the setup guide at the start of the book and have Pip installed, install Nose by running the following command:

```
$ pip install nose
...
Successfully installed nose
Cleaning up...
```

Ideally, you should do this for each Python Virtualenv you create for any projects you are working on, as opposed to installing globally. However, either approach will work. When the "Successfully installed nose" message appears, you are ready to go. It is worth pointing out that at the time of writing, the latest version of Nose to be released is 1.3.0. Usually you should try to use the latest version of a package that is available as it may have had bug fixes or new features added. However, should you wish to install the same version used to write this book you can instruct Pip to install a specific version, like so (replacing the 1.3.0 with whatever version you prefer, of course):

```
$ pip install nose==1.3.0
```

After you install Nose, you should have the `nosetests` command available to you at the terminal. Try it out by running the following command within a project that has test files which follow the naming conventions outlined in Chapter 2.

```
$ nosetests
..
-------------------------------------------------------------
Ran 2 tests in 0.010s
OK
```

Your output, similar to this, will appear to indicate your tests executed. It now should be clear why the naming conventions I explain earlier in the book are so important. Nose looks in directories for files ending `_test.py`. So if you didn't name them following that convention, Nose simply can't find them.

Using Nose's Best Features

Nose has many features and switches that you can enable on the command line to help run your tests effectively. In this section, I outline some of the best features and plug-ins to get you running your tests perfectly in no time.

Running Specific Test Files

You can run the nosetests command to search the directories for the correct test files. However, if you want to run a specific file of tests you can pinpoint the command to the file, like this:

```
$ nosetests test/calculate_test.py

----------------------------------------------------------------
Ran 2 tests in 0.003s
```

Getting More Detail with Verbose

By default Nosetests capture any output that would normally be produced when running the code, clearing away all the output in this fashion. Nosetest provides a high-level overview of the test execution, letting you focus on which tests were run and their status of passing or fail. Due to this behavior, Nosetests provides two switches that enable more information to be output when running your tests. The two switches are Verbose (-v) and No Log Capture (-s). Verbose prints out the test names to show you exactly what is being run, whereas No Log Capture enables output to reach standard out on the command line. By using this switch, you can do simple debugging using `print` statements to get more information about the state of variables, for example. To enable these two modes, you provide the -s (No Log Capture) and -v (Verbose) flags at the command line prompt. If you change the test method to print the word "Hello" and add the flags you can see the output behavior that they enable.

```
def test_add_method_returns_correct_result(self):
    print 'Hello'
    self.assertEqual(4, self.calc.add("Hello", "World"))
    self.assertAlmostEquals(1,1)


nosetests -sv test/calculate_test.py
test_add_method_raises_typeerror_if_not_ints
(test.calculate_test.TestCalculate) ... ok
test_add_method_returns_correct_result
(test.calculate_test.TestCalculate) ...
```

```
Hello
ok
----------------------------------------------------------------
Ran 2 tests in 0.001s
OK
```

In this example, a print statement—print "Hello"—is used to see if the –s flag is working correctly.

Debugging Support with PDB

Nosetests has tight integration with Python's built-in debugger PDB. PDB is a command-line debugging tool that enables you to pause your running application and interact with it while it is loaded in memory. This means you can execute Python commands to check the status of variables at the given point of stoppage. By working with your application in this way, you can often discover the cause of problems and fix your code and/or tests. You can read more on PDB in the official Python documentation at http://docs.python.org/2/library/pdb.html.

Nosetests presents you with two options for dropping into the PDB command prompt. You can either have Nosetests debug on errors, such as when exceptions are raised, or simply just on test failures. Enabling the feature is as simple as adding a flag. The flag you use depends on your situation debugger.

To find errors only, use $ nosetests --pdb. For failing tests, use $ nosetests --pdb-failures. If you change the test to fail by asserting that 2 and 2 will equal 3, then you can execute nosetests –pdb-failures to see the debugger in action.

After you have executed the command you are presented with the PDB command line. From there run the command up twice and then list, to show the few lines on either side of where the debugger is currently stopped.

```
(Pdb) up
(Pdb) up
(Pdb) list
  9
 10             def test_add_method_returns_correct_result(self):
 11                 print
 12                 print
 13                 print "Hello"
 14  ->            self.assertEqual(3, self.calc.add(2,2))
 15
```

```
16          def
test_add_method_raises_typeerror_if_not_ints(self):
17            self.assertRaises(TypeError, self.calc.add, "Hello",
"World")
18
19    if __name__ == '__main__':
 (Pdb) self.calc.add(4,4)
8
 (Pdb)
```

You can execute any Python code you like once stopped and you may want to interact with the classes loaded in the test to find out the problem (for example, `self.calc.add()` in the previous debug session).

You can read the documentation online for the full guide on using PDB, but some of the key commands to move you around your application in PDB as described in the documentation are

- `n(next)` : Continue execution until the next line in the current function is reached or it returns. (The difference between next and step is that step stops inside a called function, while next executes called functions at (nearly) full speed, only stopping at the next line in the current function.)

- `w(where)` : Print a stack trace, with the most recent frame at the bottom. An arrow indicates the current frame, which determines the context of most commands.

- `d(down)` : Move the current frame one level down in the stack trace (to a newer frame).

- `u(up)` : Move the current frame one level up in the stack trace (to an older frame).

- `b(break) [[filename:]lineno | function[, condition]]` : With a `lineno` argument, set a break there in the current file. With a `function` argument, set a break at the first executable statement within that function. The line number may be prefixed with a filename and a colon, to specify a breakpoint in another file (probably one that hasn't been loaded yet). The file is searched on `sys.path`. Note that each breakpoint is assigned a number to which all the other breakpoint commands refer.

  If a second argument is present, it is an expression, which must evaluate to true before the breakpoint is honored.

  Without argument, list all breaks, including for each breakpoint, the number of times that breakpoint has been hit, the current ignore count, and the associated condition, if any.

Checking Your Coverage

One of the key things in unit tests is having good code coverage. If large parts of your application have no unit tests, then some hidden problems may surface only in production, which is obviously a bad scenario. Fortunately, Nosetests has integration with the coverage package (you can read more about it in Chapter 9). Coverage reports basically give you a percentage for each file in your application, indicating how many lines of that file are covered by unit tests. If any lines are not covered, you can write tests to exercise those parts of your application.

By default, the Nosetest help command lists `--with-coverage` as an option. However, to enable it to work you must first install the `nose-cov` package.

```
$ pip install nose-cov
```

If you would like to install the latest version at the time of writing, you can try:

```
$ pip install nose-cov==1.6
```

This installs the coverage package alongside some integration with Nose itself. Now you can run the coverage report on the simple `Calculate.py` example to see the coverage you have on that class.

```
$ nosetests --with-coverage test/calculate_test.py
..
Name               Stmts   Miss   Cover   Missing
--------------------------------------------------
app                    1      0   100%
app.calculate         11      3    73%   13-15
--------------------------------------------------
TOTAL                 12      3    75%
------------------------------------------------------------------
Ran 2 tests in  0.001s
OK
```

The report shows that you have tested most of a file, but that some lines are not covered. Those lines are actually the code that handles the running of the application itself.

```
if __name__ == '__main__':
    calc = Calculate()
    result = calc.add(2, 2)
    print results
```

As the developer, you can make decisions about what you need to test. In this case, since the functionality is what you really want to test, these lines can be excluded from the coverage report. This feature should be used as little as possible so you get accurate information about what you are covering. In this case, it is safe to use the coverage report feature to remove lines that you know need not be tested.

```
if __name__ == '__main__': #pragma: no cover
    calc = Calculate()
    result = calc.add(2, 2)
    print results
```

Adding the comment #pragma: no cover tells the coverage tool to ignore the code on that line. If it is placed at class level or, in this case, on an if statement, the contents of that code is also removed. Now you run the report again and you should see full coverage.

```
nosetests --with-coverage test/calculate_test.py
..
Name              Stmts   Miss  Cover   Missing
-----------------------------------------------
app                   1      0   100%
app.calculate         7      0   100%
-----------------------------------------------
TOTAL                 8      0   100%
----------------------------------------------------------------
Ran 2 tests in 0.001s
OK
```

Coloring your tests with Rednose

Another useful plug-in to the Nosetests framework is Rednose. This plug-in colors your test output to indicate whether a test has passed or failed. Rednose colors passing tests green and shows failing tests and the reason for failure in red. While this is a simple addition to your workflow, it makes reading the test failures easier ; if you are running a suite of tests, picking out the failures becomes a lot easier because they show up as a block of red in your terminal.

To use Rednose, you need to install it to your Python installation or Virtualenv. Like other packages mentioned earlier, you can install Rednose using Pip.

```
$ pip install rednose
```

If you would like to install the latest version available at the time of writing, you can try:

```
$ pip install rednose==0.4.1
```

Once you have `Rednose` installed, you can then add it as an argument when running any of your tests using Nose. Nose allows chaining of these commands, so feel free to try running your tests with Coverage and `Rednose`, for example.

```
$ nosetests --rednose
```

PyTest: An Alternative Test Runner

PyTest is another popular test runner for Python and indeed is as mature and feature rich as Nose for running your tests. Which one you choose to use in your own projects is merely a personal preference or perhaps based on the use of a plug-in for a specific reason, which may be available in only one of the runners. Whichever you decide to use, both test runners are mature and dependable packages for helping automate, run, and debug your tests.

Installing PyTest

PyTest is a command-line utility that you can execute to run your tests. To get the runner installed on your system, you simply need to use Pip.

```
$ pip install pytest
...
Successfully installed pytest py
Cleaning up...
```

At the time of writing, the current latest version of PyTest is 2.5.1, released on December 17, 2013. The package is well maintained and has regular updates to add features and remove bugs.

Should you wish to install this specific version, then simply provide the fixed version to Pip, like so:

```
$ pip install pytest==2.5.1
```

Fortunately, PyTest supports the same test structure as Nose, and therefore, any tests you have written in the style outlined in this book should be picked up by the PyTest runner. To check whether this is the case, run PyTest on your tests to see if they run.

```
$ py.test
================================================================
= test session starts
================================================================
platform darwin -- Python 2.7.5 -- pytest-2.5.1
collected 2 items

test/calculate_test.py ..
================================================================
2 passed in 0.06 seconds
================================================================
```

As you can see, like Nose, the PyTest runner has collected the two tests you have in your example project from `calculate_test.py`. A nice feature of the PyTest runner, which is in contrast to Nose, is the listing of the test file location. The dots next to the filename indicate how many tests it ran. This is useful for ensuring it has picked up the directories and files you are expecting.

PyTest's Best Features

PyTest comes with many features as part of its ability to execute your tests. Just like Nosetest it offers many options that you can use as part of running your tests to give you more help and guidance as to the execution status of your tests. Outlined in this section are some of the best features that PyTest provides.

Running Specific Tests

Like Nose, PyTest can target specific tests to execute, which is useful, particularly when you are working on a specific part of your application and don't want to execute the entire test suite. To specify a test target, simply provide the path to the test file to run as the first argument to the PyTest runner.

```
$ py.test test/calculate_test.py
================================================================
test session starts
================================================================
platform darwin -- Python 2.7.5 -- pytest-2.5.1
collected 2 items

test/calculate_test.py ..

================================================================
2 passed in 0.02 seconds
================================================================
```

Viewing Detail with Verbose and Summary

PyTest provides options to get more detail on the tests you are running and information on failing tests to help you zero in on the problem quicker. The first choice developers look for when wanting extra detail is to enable verbose mode. Verbose (-v) adds extra information, such as the test filename, class name, and line number of the failing test. If you cause the add method test in `calculate_test.py` to expect 2 and 2 to add up to 3 you can see how PyTest can give information on failing tests.

```
$ py.test -v
==================================================================
= test session starts
==================================================================
platform darwin -- Python 2.7.5 -- pytest-2.5.1 --
/Users/username/.virtualenvs/python_testing/bin/python
collected 2 items

test/calculate_test.py:13:
TestCalculate.test_add_method_raises_typeerror_if_not_ints
 PASSED
test/calculate_test.py:10:
 TestCalculate.test_add_method_returns_correct_result FAILED


==================================================================
== FAILURES
==================================================================
==

_____

TestCalculate.test_add_method_returns_correct_result

_____

self = <test.calculate_test.TestCalculate
testMethod=test_add_method_returns_correct_result>

    def test_add_method_returns_correct_result(self):
>       self.assertEqual(3, self.calc.add(2,2))
E       AssertionError: 3 != 4

test/calculate_test.py:11: AssertionError
==============================================================
1 failed, 1 passed in 0.03 seconds
==============================================================
```

PyTest also provides the option to output extra test summary information. Essentially, this option lists the names of the tests that are failing and is good for getting a quick list of exactly which test files you need to investigate. Using this feature can be particularly helpful when you have a large project with many test files: This can help you get to the files quickly and easily.

The extra test summary option is enabled by the −r flag to the PyTest command, followed by one of the following letters:

- f (failed)
- E (error)
- s (skipped)
- x (failed)
- X (passed)

For example, here is the output PyTest will provide if you use the failed flag. PyLint returns just the names of the failing tests, line numbers of where the fail occurred and the type of error that caused the failure.

```
$ py.test -r f
...
test/calculate_test.py:11: AssertionError
================================================================
short test summary info
================================================================
FAIL
test/calculate_test.py::TestCalculate::test_add_method_returns_
correct_result
==========================================================
1 failed, 1 passed in 0.03 seconds
==========================================================
```

Debugging with PDB

PyTest offers integration with Python's built-in debug tool, PDB. In an almost identical style to Nose, you can drop into the Python Debugger whenever your test fails to extract information on the application at run time and while loaded in memory. A subtle difference to the way Nose handles PDB is that you will drop into the debug command prompt on any type of failure, either an assertion error or exception being raised, for example. With Nose, you must specify under which situation you want to use PDB. Enabling the option is as simple as adding the -pdb flag to the command line runner. So for example if you change the test method in calculate_test.py to raise Exception() straight away and run the Python debugger using PyTest, you can expect the following.

```
$ py.test --pdb
================================================================
= test session starts
================================================================
platform darwin -- Python 2.7.5 -- pytest-2.5.1
collected 2 items

test/calculate_test.py .F
>>>>>>>>>>>>>>>>>>>>>>>>>>>>>>>>>>>>>>>>>>>>>>>>>>>>>>>>>>>>>>>>>
>>>>>> traceback
>>>>>>>>>>>>>>>>>>>>>>>>>>>>>>>>>>>>>>>>>>>>>>>>>>>>>>>>>>>>>>>>>

self = <test.calculate_test.TestCalculate
testMethod=test_add_method_returns_correct_result>

    def test_add_method_returns_correct_result(self):
>         raise Exception()
E         Exception

test/calculate_test.py:11: Exception
>>>>>>>>>>>>>>>>>>>>>>>>>>>>>>>>>>>>>>>>>>>>>>>>>>>>>>>>>>>>>>>>>
>>>>> entering PDB
>>>>>>>>>>>>>>>>>>>>>>>>>>>>>>>>>>>>>>>>>>>>>>>>>>>>>>>>>>>>>>>>>
>>>>>
/Users/username/workspace/python_testing/test/calculate_test.py(11)
test_add_method_returns_correct_result()
-> raise Exception()
(Pdb)
```

From here, you are simply using PDB, covered in the earlier section about Nose, "Debugging Support with PDB." Refer to that section for details on using the PDB command prompt. One thing of note at this point, is that PDB will often drop you in several calls down from the actual test code. You can use the w command to see the chain of calls and use up to get to the place in the code you'd like to be, which in this case is the test file itself.

Checking Your Coverage with PyTest

PyTest provides coverage support, again via the use of a plug-in. The plug-in can be installed using Pip, so it is a virtually painless install and provides you with a great feature for keeping a check on your application test coverage. To enable the coverage feature, you must first Pip install the pytest-cov plug-in.

```
$ pip install pytest-cov
Successfully installed pytest-cov
Cleaning up...
```

Should you wish to install the specific version used at the time of writing, then simply provide the fixed version to Pip, like so:

```
$ pip install pytest-cov==1.6
```

Once this is installed, from the top-level directory of your project you need to pass in two arguments: the application folder containing your actual code and the test directory folder.

```
$ py.test --cov app/ test/
================================================================
= test session starts
================================================================
platform darwin -- Python 2.7.5 -- pytest-2.5.1
plugins: cov
collected 2 items

test/calculate_test.py ..
-------------------------------------------------- coverage:
 platform darwin, python 2.7.5-final-0 ------------------------
---------------------------
Name            Stmts   Miss   Cover
----------------------------------
app/__init__        1      0    100%
app/calculate       7      0    100%
----------------------------------
TOTAL               8      0    100%


================================================================
2 passed in 0.03 seconds
 ================================================================
```

You can configure the coverage report to omit certain files or folders, if you choose. For example, in the preceding output, you have a coverage report for the package, indicating __init__.py files. Although it is showing as 100%, you don't really need or want it to appear in your report. Fortunately, you can configure the coverage report using a .coveragerc file. To remove all __init__.py files, create a file named .coveragerc in the root directory of your project and add the following:

```
[run]
omit=*__init__.py
```

Now whenever you run the tests with coverage, these files will be ignored. You can specify directories or files and also use wildcards to match patterns that you want to ignore.

Choosing Between Nose and PyTest

Throughout this chapter, I clearly outline the similarity of the two test runners. Either package is a great choice for use in your project; it mostly comes down to a decision of preference on the style of output from the runners and how to use the features that you prefer. Should a plug-in from the vast array provided for each runner exist only for one, then that may sway your decision, but the coverage plug-in, for example, shows that there is great support in the Python community for both of these mature, established testing frameworks. It's also worth noting that both frameworks allow you to write test methods within a class and not inherit from unittest.TestCase. Should you wish to write more custom testing suites, this allows you the flexibility to do so without being tied to the structures and principles that the standard unittest module provides. More information can be found on the official websites for each package, where you can find detailed documentation and support.

- **Nosetests:** http://nose.readthedocs.org/en/latest/
- **PyTest:** http://pytest.org/latest/

Mock and Patch Tricky Situations

When you write tests, you may discover that your code interacts with other systems that are assumed to be tested and fully functional, such as call a database or a web service. In these instances, you don't want to make those calls for real in your test—for a number of reasons. For example, the database or web service may be down and you don't want that to cause a failing test as part of your build process, which would produce a false positive. Also, those calls may be slow or cost your company money; therefore, if you are running a build every time you check in, your build could get lengthy or cost the company a large bill. This is where mocking and patching come in. They enable you to swap those real calls for dummy responses. This allows you to test that your code behaves as expected under those conditions.

Installing the Mock Library

Before you begin, you must install the Mock library so that you can create mock instances of the classes you want to create dummy responses for. To do this simply, Pip install the package as you have done before.

```
$ pip install mock
...
Successfully installed mock
Cleaning up...
```

For information purposes, the Mock library was at version 1.0.1 at the time of writing and was updated on November 5, 2013. The library is relatively mature and should be considered a stable release, as denoted by its use of a major version number in 1.0.

Mocking a Class and Method Response

Creating a mock is fairly simple. You simply need to import the Mock class and then create an instance of it. You can then attach methods to the mock that you want to return some value. Create a test file called mock_example_test.py and use the following code.

```python
import unittest
from mock import Mock


class TestMocking(unittest.TestCase):
    def test_mock_method_returns(self):
        my_mock = Mock()
        my_mock.my_method.return_value = "hello"
        self.assertEqual("hello", my_mock.my_method())

if __name__ == '__main__':
    unittest.main()
```

In this example, you can create an instance of the mock named my_mock, add the my_method to it, and state that when it is called, it should return the string "hello".

You may now wonder how this is useful when testing your application. Suppose you have a program that looks up accounts from a database. If that account class is initialized using a data_interface class to call a database for the account information, then instead of providing a real data_interface you can instead mock the data_interface and provide the methods and return values you need for your test. Because the data_interface class is a whole other class with set responsibilities, the testing for this class should be assumed as handled elsewhere. To that end, the mock `data_interface` will just be set up to have a dummy method on it and return whatever you like when it is called. This allows you to set up the scenarios and use cases of the code as required, such as returning a value successfully for an account or returning some error case.

To illustrate this example with some code, your simple Account class may look something like this:

```
class Account(object):
    def __init__(self, data_interface):
        self.di = data_interface

    def get_account(self, id_num):
        return self.di.get(id_num)
```

The class has just one method that returns the data obtained from the database related to the provided ID number. Now write a test to check that the data is returned correctly for ID 1 given the data that you set up in the mock `data_interface`. Create a test file called `account_test.py` and try the following code:

```
import unittest
from mock import Mock
from app.account import Account


class TestAccount(unittest.TestCase):
    def test_account_returns_data_for_id_1(self):
        account_data = {"id": "1", "name": "test"}
        mock_data_interface = Mock()
mock_data_interface.get.return_value = account_data
        account = Account(mock_data_interface)
        self.assertDictEqual(account_data,
 account.get_account(1))


if __name__ == '__main__':
    unittest.main()
```

By passing in the `mock_data_interface` in this way, you can create the scenario you need to exercise only the Account class without testing any of the functionality provided by the `data_interface` class.

Now that you have control over the scenarios the class can experience, you can test for eventualities such as exception handling by mocking that an exception was raised when calling the `data_interface` layer. Being able to handle these types of cases is powerful and one of the main driving forces behind the test driven development approach (see Chapter 5).

The `get_account` method changes to handle an exception that in this case is a custom error called `ConnectionError`. This is defined in the code as:

```
class ConnectionError(Exception):
    pass
```

The method is then updated to check for the error that could occur and returns an error message, like so:

```
def get_account(self, id_num):
    try:
        result = self.di.get(id_num
    except ConnectionError:
        result = "Connection error occurred. Try Again."
    return result
```

You can then test that this code handles the exception and returns the correct error message by mocking the raising of the exception when calling the `data_interface` layer. Add the following test method to your `account_test.py` test file.

```
def test_account_when_connect_exception_raised(self):
    mock_data_interface = Mock()
    mock_data_interface.get.side_effect = ConnectionError()
    account = Account(mock_data_interface)
    self.assertEqual("Connection error occurred. Try Again.",
        account.get_account(1))
```

This full control over the code means you remove this reliance on the real database, and bring elements under your control to ensure the code is tested to your standards. Testing in this level of isolation is useful later down the line in performance testing, where you want to limit or eradicate external factors so that you can test just your code in isolation, providing a true indication of the performance of your code. For more on this, see Chapter 8.

When Mock Won't Do, Patch!

Sometimes your application is designed in such a way that mocking just isn't applicable or won't work. These instances most often occur when you import some library or your own code to perform a function but don't want to call the real code in the test. If there is no way of injecting the mock, like in the previous example, then you must "patch" the code to replace the real instance with an instance of Mock. Once you have applied the patch, the method of setting up the return values is the same as in the Mock example.

The Requests Library

A classic example of a library in use that you do not want to test would be the `requests` library. This robust library has become popular among Python developers who want to call web services, and in particular, REST services (for example, GET, POST, PUT, DELETE, and so forth). The `requests` library is a wrapper around the Python standard library utility `urllib2`. Therefore, to be able to use the requests library and follow these examples, you must first Pip install `requests`.

```
$ pip install requests
Successfully installed requests
Cleaning up...
```

As I noted earlier, the version used at the time of writing is 2.1.0; if that's the version you want to use, simply append the version number when installing, like so:

```
$ pip install requests==2.1.0
```

Patch in Action

As in the database example, you do not want to call these real web services in your tests, because while you are running the tests these services may be unavailable or a network outage may cause intermittent test failures that have nothing to do with the code.

To patch a library such as this, you can use the `@patch` decorator, and specify the *target* you want to patch with a Mock instance. The documentation describes *target* as:

"*Target* should be a string in the form *'package.module.ClassName'*. The *target* is imported and the specified object replaced with the *new* object, so the *target* must be importable from the environment you are calling *patch* from. The target is imported when the decorated function is executed, not at decoration time."

To illustrate the use of patch, add a method to your `Account` class that makes use of a `requests.get` call to a web service to obtain some data.

```
import requests
...
    def get_current_balance(self, id_num):
        return requests.get("http://some-account-uri/"+id_num)
```

The requests to your web service append the `id_num` of the account to look up that specific account's details. From there, you simply return the data that is obtained from the GET request to that URL. Now if you want to test that when the method is called and you get a successful response from the GET request, the data is returned to you, and you need to apply the patch on the requests library.

```
import unittest
from mock import Mock, patch
from app.account import Account


class TestAccount(unittest.TestCase):
    @patch('app.account.requests')
    def test_get_current_balance_returns_data_correctly(self,
            mock_requests):
        mock_requests.get.return_value = '500'
        account = Account(Mock())
        self.assertEqual('500', account.get_current_balance('1'))
```

You may notice that you still use `Mock` in this example, but that is merely so you could create an instance of the `Account` class, which requires a `data_interface` object. In this case, you can just provide a `Mock`; it is not used after the initialization of your class. This demonstrates another good use of `Mock`, when you do not care what an object is being used for and does not influence the testing of your code. Sometimes mocks used in this way are called dummies.

Other points of note from the example are the way in which you target the requests library. It is important that you target the instance of requests imported in your `Account` class file and not just `@patch('requests')`, which will not work. You must be specific with the target and specify the actual file in which the library under patch is imported.

Once patched, the mock instance is passed through to the test as the first argument after `self`. From that point forward, you can treat your `mock` instance exactly as before. You can mock the `get` call you perform in your code and complete the test to see that the method does indeed return the value obtained from the request.

It is important to keep your tests as specific and unique as possible. Testing one aspect of your code and one thing only helps to keep maintenance of your tests low. Having such succinct tests allows for easy debugging when tests fail as they should each have only one piece of functionality that they are testing, narrowing down the problem significantly. Mocking and patching help you to achieve this by eliminating the code that is superfluous to the code under test. You gain isolation of your code and the ability to narrow down on one aspect of its functionality with each test at a time.

Advanced Mocking

With a little knowledge about the request library, you can take this example a step further and undertake some better mocking of the real requests library behavior. As a developer who has used the library, you will know that when you perform a GET request such as this, the library returns an object with certain properties, such as `status_code` and `text` among others. Change your `Account` class to make use of these properties so that you can then patch the behavior in your test.

```python
def get_current_balance(self, id_num):
    response = requests.get("http://some-account-uri/"+id_num)
    return {'status': response.status_code,
            'data': response.text}
```

With the newly updated code, your test from earlier would fail as you simply mock the library to return a string. What you need to do now is make the mock request return a second mock. You can then attach the properties to the second mock to mimic the behavior of the requests library.

```python
@patch('app.account.requests')
def test_get_current_balance_returns_data_correctly(self,
        mock_requests):
    mock_response = Mock()
    mock_response.status_code = 200
    mock_response.text = 'Some text data'
    mock_requests.get.return_value = mock_response
    account = Account(Mock())
    self.assertEqual({'status': 200, 'data': 'Some text data'},
                     account.get_current_balance('1'))
```

Notice how you create the `mock_response` object first, adding in the properties you need and then set the `return_value` of the `mock_request.get` call to return your `mock_response`. Now you have the mock and patch in place to be able to test all the different scenarios that HTTP calls present, such as getting a 404 Not Found, or 500 Bad Server, and handling those situations in your code.

Summary

In this chapter, you took your testing to the next level. Adding tools to your daily workflow makes the processes of running tests easier and debugging a breeze. The use of well developed, standardized tools among the Python community ensures that becoming proficient using one or both of the Nose and PyTest tools is a worthwhile exercise and essential as part of any modern Agile (see Chapter 5) development team and build process.

The vast array of plug-ins available for these tools means that whatever it is you're testing and whatever stats, extra information, or integration with other toolsets you need is likely already there. Should you find it isn't, then solid documentation around both tools will guide you on what you need to do.

You then took to the Mock library and the testing possibilities and improvements these make to your applications test suite. The capability to isolate code and mock behavior of external code and libraries is valuable and ensures you test only the code you write and care about at this specific point in the application's development.

Mock and patch allow you to avoid test failure headaches caused by real service issues such as network problems, downtime, and cost agreements. Mocking gives you control over the situations you want to test your application in; with this control, you can ensure that your application's code is covered from all angles you expect it to encounter.

Chapter 4
Writing Testable Documentation

DOCUMENTING CODE IS a process that is considered difficult. On the one hand, extensive, in-depth documentation can benefit programmers using your code greatly. It can provide examples on how to use an API, for example, or design decisions explaining why the code behaves as it does. Alternatively, as code evolves, often quite rapidly, documentation quickly can become out of date and be rendered almost useless.

Fortunately, there is a happy medium. Documentation doesn't need to be in the form of a huge document or website. It can be a combination of short formal documents (such as a website or wiki page), doc strings in methods, comments in code, and most importantly, the code itself. If your code follows good practices such as clear naming conventions and consistent use of styles, you can keep comments and documentation to a minimum. Adhering to best practices makes it clear to the reader what the code is doing, without the need for extra comments. That is not to say that comments and doc strings should never be used. Rather, they should be used sparingly and only on occasions that warrant their use, such as with a complicated method, or to explain why some code needed to be written a certain way or simply to offer useful information that you cannot convey in the method names and code you write. By keeping comments to a minimum, you avoid having out-of-date documentation. Maintaining the few locations requiring comments and documentation is then a much easier job.

But what if you could take it a step further, and actually have living documentation that tests the methods they are describing? What if you then build these tests into your build suite, so that if that method's behavior changes, the documentation test fails and you are forced to update the documentation? This is exactly what Python's doctest library can provide and this chapter looks to familiarize you with writing doctests, incorporating them into your daily test flow, and integrating with the toolset you have been using.

Writing Your First Doctest

The doctest module is included in the Python standard library, so you should not need to install anything to start writing a doctest. Doctest approaches the testing of your methods in a slightly different way than the unit tests you have looked at so far. Rather than using explicit methods to check the return value or exception raised by your method, you essentially provide an example of using the method in a Python shell and its expected output. With the doctests in place, you can then execute them in much the same way as unit test, as part of your daily testing suite. The doctests will pass and fail like unit tests if the expected output you express in the doctest does not match what happens when executed in a Python shell.

The Python Shell

The Python shell is basically an interactive prompt, which you can use to execute Python code and see the result. Open up a command prompt ("Terminal" on OS X and Linux), type **python**, press Enter to run the Python shell, and try the following:

```
$ python
Python 2.7.6 (default, Jan  7 2014, 12:15:04)
[GCC 4.2.1 Compatible Apple LLVM 5.0 (clang-500.2.79)] on Darwin
          Type "help", "copyright", "credits" or "license" for
  more
information.
>>>
```

When you see the >>> prompt, you can start typing Python code, like this:

```
>>> 1 + 1
2
>>>
```

The Python shell naturally allows you to execute a Python method and see the results straightaway in the shell. Create a method in the shell that takes two numbers and adds them together; call the method and then view the result:

```
>>> def add(x, y):
...     return x + y
...
>>> add(1,1)
2
>>>
```

Now that you get the basics of how the Python shell works, you can apply the same logic to create simple doctests for any methods you write.

Adding Doctests to a Method

Using the Calculator example from Chapter 2, you can go ahead and add some doc strings to explain what the methods are doing. Again, for those unfamiliar with the concept, doc strings are usually triple-quoted strings placed directly under the method name to explain the method's responsibilities.

```
def my_method_with_docstring(arg):
    """This is my doc string.  Here you would describe what the
    method is doing."""
```

Doctest extends these strings to include examples of the method in use. Apply a doc string to your add method in the Calculate class from Chapter 2.

```
    def add(self, x, y):
        """Takes two integers and adds them together to produce
        the result."""

        if type(x) == int and type(y) == int:
            return x + y
        else:
            raise TypeError("Invalid type: {} and        {}"
                .format(type(x), type(y)))
```

The method now clearly describes its intentions to the reader. You now can add some example use cases of the method to show the expected behavior to the reader, and then run them as doctests. Add some examples where you pass in only integers.

```
    def add(self, x, y):
        """Takes two integers and adds them together to produce
        the result.

        >>> c = Calculate()
        >>> c.add(1, 1)
        2

        >>> c.add(25, 125)
        150
        """

        if type(x) == int and type(y) == int:
            return x + y
```

```
        else:
            raise TypeError("Invalid type: {} and {}"
                .format(type(x), type(y)))
```

Notice how you create an instance of the class `Calculate`, to then be able to call your method and show the expected output. This replicates exactly what you would need to do in the Python shell, so if you are ever unsure of what to place in your doctest, simply try it out in the shell first.

Running Your Doctests

At present, there is no way you can execute the doctest. To enable it to run, you must first add a block of code that will execute when you run the Python file containing this class. Add the following to the bottom of the file.

```
if __name__ == "__main__":
    import doctest
    doctest.testmod()
```

Now when you execute the file, you should receive no output. This is a little counterintuitive, but it means that the test passed and the method behaves as expected.

```
$ python app/calculate.py
$
```

To be sure that your doctests are actually being executed, you can add a verbose flag, `-v`, to see information about what tests are being run.

```
$ python app/calculate.py -v
Trying:
    c = Calculate()
Expecting nothing
ok
Trying:
    c.add(1, 1)
Expecting:
    2
ok
Trying:
    c.add(25, 125)
Expecting:
    150
```

```
ok
2 items had no tests:
    __main__
    __main__.Calculate
1 items passed all tests:
   3 tests in __main__.Calculate.add
3 tests in 3 items.
3 passed and 0 failed.
Test passed.
```

The output from doctest is quite nice, showing clearly each line it is executing from your doctest, what it is expecting from this line, and whether it passed. When doctest fails, you also get detailed information as to why. Change the expectation of add(1, 1) to 3 without the verbose flag. You will be told about the failing doctest.

```
$ python app/calculate.py
**********************************************************************
File "app/calculate.py", line 10, in __main__.Calculate.add
Failed example:
    c.add(1, 1)
Expected:
    3
Got:
    2
**********************************************************************
1 items had failures:
   1 of   3 in __main__.Calculate.add
***Test Failed*** 1 failures.
```

You clearly are shown the line that caused the issue, what was expected, and what it actually returned. You can then either update your tests to be correct or change the behavior of your method that has caused the failing test. Again, you can use the -v flag to get even more information and see the line-by-line detail.

Handling Error Cases

You can, of course, demonstrate error cases to the reader, showing conditions that cause your method to throw an exception and testing to prove that is indeed what will happen. The Python documentation for doctest states that you can test for an exception being raised *provided that the traceback is the only output produced by the example*. It also is worth noting that a traceback contains many dynamic elements that can be omitted within your doctest. For example, the traceback usually contains lots of file paths that are specific to the code running on your machine.

This can be best illustrated using the error scenario in your add method. The add method supports the addition of only two integers. If you pass a float to the method, a TypeError is raised. Add the following doctest to the doc string to check that the exception is thrown in this scenario.

```
def add(self, x, y):
    """Takes two integers and adds them together to produce
    the result.

    >>> c = Calculate()
    >>> c.add(1.0, 1.0)
    Traceback (most recent call last):
     ...
    TypeError: Invalid type: <type 'float'> and <type \
    'float'>
    """
    if type(x) == int and type(y) == int:
        return x + y
    else:
        raise TypeError("Invalid type: {} and {}"
            .format(type(x), type(y)))
```

When you are expecting an exception to be raised, you must start the result with Traceback (most recent call last): or Traceback (innermost last): depending on how the exception is raised in your code. Then you can ignore the body of the traceback that will be dependent on the machine you are running on using an ellipsis (. . .). The last line indicates the actual exception you expect to be raised, including the error message. When you run this now, initially there will be no output as the test passes.

```
$ python app/calculate.py
$
```

Running the doctests with the verbose flag confirms that the exception test has indeed been executed correctly.

```
$ python app/calculate.py -v
Trying:
    c = Calculate()
Expecting nothing
ok
Trying:
    c.add(1.0, 1.0)
Expecting:
    Traceback (most recent call last):
      ...
    TypeError: Invalid type: <type 'float'> and <type 'float'>
ok
3 items had no tests:
    __main__
    __main__.Calculate
    __main__.Calculate.__init__
1 items passed all tests:
   4 tests in __main__.Calculate.add
4 tests in 4 items.
4 passed and 0 failed.
Test passed.
```

Advanced Doctest Usage

If you are not smart about the doctests you write, they can quickly become quite large and distract from the actual code you write. The code should always be given the priority and be the focus for the reader. However succinct, descriptive examples of the method can provide context for the method to the developer reading the code. Fortunately, you can apply some tricks to your doctests to reduce the amount of code you need to write in them.

In the Calculate example, your method is part of the class. Because of this fact, when you write your doctests you must first create an instance of the `Calculate` class, store this in a variable, and then call your method as expected. In a class with many methods, creating this instance every time can be tedious and take up valuable space for the doctest and code. The doctest module allows for a context to be passed in, which is then available to all doctests in the file. So instead of creating the instance `c = Calculate()` every time, you can do this just once in the doctest runner.

```python
if __name__ == "__main__":
    import doctest
    doctest.testmod(extraglobs={'c': Calculate()})
```

With this improvement in place, the need to create your class instance within the doctests themselves is removed and keeps the code cleaner as follows:

```
def add(self, x, y):
        """Takes two integers and adds them together to produce the
  result.

        >>> c.add(1,1)
        2

        >>> c.add(25,125)
        150

        >>> c.add(1.0, 1.0)
        Traceback (most recent call last):
          ...
        TypeError: Invalid type: <type 'float'> and <type 'float'>
        """
        if type(x) == int and type(y) == int:
            return x + y
        else:
            raise TypeError("Invalid type: {} and
  {}".format(type(x), type(y)))
```

Improving Doctests with Nose Integration

Running doctests by executing the Python file they are in is an okay process for testing in this style, but what if you start to expand your doctests to many classes and methods? Also, running the tests as part of a build process will be difficult to manage should you need to maintain a list of which files to execute that contain doctests.

Fortunately, you can make use of some tight integration with the nosetest runner, which was introduced earlier in the book. Nosetest provides a way of appending a flag to your normal nosetest command, which searches through the files for doctests and executes them. This enables you to run doctests with all the convenient features that you were introduced to earlier, such as colorized output, debugging, and clear, readable stack traces that explain why the doctests failed.

You enable the nose's doctest support by running the `nosetests` command with the flag `-with-doctest`. `Nosetests` then searches all the files for doctests and executes them alongside your unit tests (refer to Chapters 2 and 3) and acceptance tests (refer to Chapters 6 and 7).

Running the `nosetests` command on its own runs just your two unit tests for the `Calculate` class.

```
$ nosetests
.........................
-----------------------------------------------------------------
Ran 2 tests in 0.064s
OK
```

Now when you add the option for doctest, it picks up the doctest you wrote for the `add` method on the `Calculate` class. Note at this point, if you have your doctests set up to use `extraglob` as shown a few pages earlier, `nosetest` will fail at this point. This is due to the fact that the `extraglob` directive is set in __main__, which is not called by the `nosetest` runner. For this reason, you need to undo the changes made to support `extraglob`, mainly creating an instance of the class within your doctest, to proceed with `nosetest`.

```
$ nosetests --with-doctest
.........................
-----------------------------------------------------------------
Ran 3 tests in 0.064s
OK
```

To confirm this is indeed the case, you can add the verbose flag so that nosetest informs you about exactly what it is executing.

```
$ nosetests --with-doctest -v
Doctest: app.calculate.Calculate.add ... ok
test_add_method_raises_typeerror_if_not_ints
  (test.calculate_test.TestCalculate) ... ok
test_add_method_returns_correct_result
  (test.calculate_test.TestCalculate) ... ok
```

The doctest that was run is clearly marked by nosetest as a `"Doctest"`.

Finally, if you make the doctest fail, such as using the add method to expect 1 add 1 to equal 3, nosetest will clearly indicate where and why a problem has occurred.

```
$ nosetests --with-doctest
F..
================================================================
FAIL: Doctest: app.calculate.Calculate.add
----------------------------------------------------------------
Traceback (most recent call last):
  File
"/usr/local/Cellar/python/2.7.5/Frameworks/Python.framework/Vers
ions/2.7/lib/python2.7/doctest.py", line 2201, in runTest
    raise
self.failureException(self.format_failure(new.getvalue()))
AssertionError: Failed doctest test for
app.calculate.Calculate.add
  File "/Users/username/workspace/python_testing/app/calculate.py",
 line 6, in add


----------------------------------------------------------------


File "/Users/username/workspace/python_testing/app/calculate.py",
 line 10, in app.calculate.Calculate.add
Failed example:
    c.add(1,1)
Expected:
    3
Got:
    2



----------------------------------------------------------------
Ran 3 tests in 0.064s
FAILED (failures=1)
```

The section in bold outlines the detail that nosetest will give you. It pinpoints the line number, file, class, and method involved and shows you the arguments to the method along with what was expected and the actual result. This allows you to either fix the code that caused the problem or update your test with confidence. You should be running your tests frequently after each change to either the test or code. By running frequently, you keep changes that can affect the outcome of the test to a minimum, making it easier to identify problems and rectify them.

Summary

In this chapter, you were introduced to the concept of documentation testing in Python. By building in documentation that can actually test your implementation, you ensure that the documentation remains up to date, as changes to the code would force changes to the doctests. The doctests you write provide developers not only with an explanation of what a method is doing, but also an indication of its usage and expected results when called.

You looked at examples of writing a doctest and how it ties in closely to the Python shell where you can execute Python code and see the result. The examples also provided the means to execute the doctests to see if your code actually passes the tests that you have written. You learned how to test the positive uses of your methods and also the error cases where exceptions are raised, showing how those can be handled in a doctest.

The final part of the chapter focused on incorporating your doctests into a daily development cycle in running them with automated test tools such as Nose. The integration with Nose provides better output when running the tests, and increased readability when the tests fail, making debugging what went wrong easier. I also covered some optimizations to your doctests such as ways to create instances of your classes once keeping the lines in your test to a minimum, helping to maintain readability.

Resources

Doctest Documentation: `https://docs.python.org/2/library/doctest.html`

Doctest Nose Integration: `http://nose.readthedocs.org/en/latest/plugins/doctests.html`

Chapter 5

Driving Your Development with Tests

THIS CHAPTER INTRODUCES the programming concept of test driven development (TDD)—a style of development that enables you to focus on testing your application and ensuring it delivers the features and functionality that you set out to create. TDD gives you great confidence that each new piece of functionality you write in your code is backed by a test, which confirms how it behaves.

Test driven development is often a key part of the agile development process, which advocates iterative development over more restrictive processes such as waterfall. TDD in agile makes testing your focus up front, rather than an afterthought at the end of development. This chapter introduces you to the ideas and concepts of agile development. It also covers the basics of how you undertake TDD, where it fits into the agile process, and the advantages of working in this way. And finally, the chapter leads you through an example in a TDD manner.

Agile Development

Agile is a process that has become increasing popular in recent years, both in personal or smaller projects and within large business such as BSkyB, Facebook, Spotify, and Netflix, to name a few. But why are the big companies moving to such a process and what benefits does it bring? The main driver behind agile development is that it is an iterative process (usually in cycles of two to four weeks), with a working deliverable at the end of each iteration. A big plus point to this process is that it removes the pressure of deadlines to some degree and teams can work to deliver a minimum viable product within a certain time frame. Basically this means you deliver the smallest product that you could release to customers that would add business value. Once you have developed this product, you can then continue to iterate and add more features. It's easy to see how this can be viewed as a more stable process for delivering software than in the waterfall method, which effectively has one "big bang" release after many weeks/months/years of development.

The agile manifesto was drafted in February 2001. It aimed to offer guidance and explain the fundamentals of the agile development process. The manifesto resulted in the following 12 principles:

- Increasing customer satisfaction by rapid delivery of useful software
- Accommodating changing requirements, even late in development
- Delivering working software frequently (weeks rather than months)
- Using working software as the principal measure of progress
- Building a sustainable development process and being able to maintain a constant pace
- Providing close, daily cooperation between business people and developers
- Communicating through face-to-face conversation, which is the best form of communication (co-location)
- Building projects around motivated individuals who should be trusted
- Paying continuous attention to technical excellence and good design
- Exercising simplicity—the art of maximizing the amount of work not done
- Creating self-organizing teams
- Making regular adaptations to changing circumstances

The key words within this list are along the lines of *working, quality, satisfaction, sustainable,* and *simplicity.* This should outline the real need for the focus on testing and following a TDD approach to your development. By working in this way, you can meet the goals of your project and follow the preceding list of principles.

Adopting the Agile Process Now

Taking up the agile process is not as difficult as it may seem. The process is effectively centered on a few key pillar concepts. The average iteration in an agile team is known as a "sprint." The topic of agile is huge and is a book in its own right, with many available on the market at present. My goal here is to give you a taste.

As mentioned earlier, the average sprint length is usually two to four weeks. In that time, the following processes must take place.

1. **Sprint planning/planning games:** Here the development team is presented with a series of stories (business requirements for the application being developed). Team members discuss how difficult the story is and what it will entail. They award story points, which are often some form of scale indicating easier to harder pieces of work. Often this is achieved by playing planning poker. Following the discussion, after a count of three the developers show the number of points they believe the story should be. The points should indicate the effort against complexity that it will take to deliver this functionality. After everyone has shown their points, a discussion follows between the developers providing the lowest and highest points. Another round of showing points may occur until a compromise can be agreed upon for the points for this story. Story points are a relative indicator of how difficult a story is. For example, a 1 may be relatively simple, whereas an 8 may have multiple parts to it, or be something difficult that the team hasn't faced before. Often teams use values from the Fibonacci scale, to allocate story points. Some teams use other units of measurement, such as man days (how long for one person to complete), pair days (how long for a pair to complete), or t-shirt sizes (for example, small, medium, large). Whichever you choose, stick to one unit of measurement; after a few iterations, your sizing of stories will settle down and start to give you an accurate estimation of what you can realistically achieve in one sprint (known as velocity).

2. **Development:** Stories can then be picked up from the agile board, which is typically a whiteboard displayed somewhere near the development team and that is split into sections to show the progress of any one story card. A usual split for a board such as this would be Sprint Backlog, In Progress, QA/Test, and Done. A developer will pick up a card from the Backlog and move it to the In Progress column. Team members will usually place some form of indicator (such as initials/avatars/monikers that represent themselves) on the card to show who is working on it. Ideally the card will be worked on in pairs who will follow the TDD approach to complete the work. When the developers are happy the card is complete, they move it to the QA/Test column, where the Quality Assurance (QA) personnel on the team can write more tests, perform manual tests, and possibly performance test the work to their satisfaction. The card can then be marked as complete and moved to the Done column and the process starts again.

3. **Showcase:** An important part of the process, as mentioned previously, is to deliver a "working" product at the end of each sprint. The term "working" is used loosely here, in that it does not mean complete or ready for the end user. Simply, it means that some functionality of the overall application is now complete or ready to be iterated on further. Any part of your project that was developed in this sprint and that can be shown to the stakeholders should be presented at the showcase. The showcase can take any form it needs to in able to demonstrate effectively the functionality that has been delivered in your project to your stakeholders. Often, this will involve a pair from the development team or analyst talking through the feature whilst demonstrating live via a projector the application in use. Ideally, showcasing should take place at the same time, and place for each sprint and demonstrate clearly what has been built and why.

4. **Retrospective:** The final pillar of the agile process is the retrospective, which takes place at the end of a sprint. The retrospective is some dedicated time for the team to reflect on the previous sprint and talk about things that went wrong, went well, or could have been different. The retrospective usually produces some useful actions for the next sprint and these should be recorded, allocated to a team member to undertake, and discussed at the next retrospective.

Ethos of Test Driven Development

The real ethos behind TDD is to give you—the developer—and your stakeholder (owner of the project) confidence in the code and application that is delivered. It ensures a high level of quality as you are forced to think about the problem at hand and cover each case with a test to prove the functionality works as expected.

The basic concept of TDD is to write a failing test first, ***before*** writing any code. You may ask how can I write a test before I know what it does? Indeed, this is a valid question that will hopefully become clearer over the course of the chapter. Essentially, the tests should drive your development by failing in a way that allows you to write a piece of code. For example, if you need a class to represent some data, and a method to access that data, then a test could call this new method on the class as if it existed. Then your test would fail indicating that the method and class do not exist and you can begin developing them. The tests guide your development, making you think about their exact behavior and responsibilities before you actually write any code.

This is key to the whole process and has a few different purposes. Writing your test first forces you to think about the problem you are trying to solve in code. Take the calculator example used so far in the book. You needed to write an add method to add together two numbers. Now, you could consider the test case where you add two numbers together and get the right result. But what if the user enters two strings? Do you support this behavior? If not, should the application respond by throwing an exception? These are some of the questions that can quickly arise when you are writing a test for even the smallest part of functionality. You can then put in place as many tests as you need to cover the different scenarios that might arise.

You may now be wondering how many tests you should be writing. What is complete coverage of the functionality? How many tests are "enough" tests? These are fair comments and can be a little overwhelming at first. However your approach to testing should be to learn and develop your techniques as you write more tests. What experienced developers often find is that if too many bugs are getting through to your released code in production, then you have not got enough coverage in your tests for all the scenarios your code faces.

On the other hand, if it becomes very difficult to make even small changes to your application (because the changes cause many tests to fail, which require updating) then you probably have too many tests. Over time you will develop a feeling for what you should be testing and the right amount of coverage some functionality requires. When writing new code you will find you often test the functionality manually anyway, and therefore your testing should be a formalization of this process, which can be reused and replayed as many times as required.

The two cases outlined here are often called the "happy" and "unhappy" paths, where the application behaves correctly or has some kind of error or problem. By taking the time to think in this way, you can define some of the edge cases (unlikely, unusual behavior) for the application. If you dive straight into the code, you may end up just covering the "happy" path through the code and not consider these extra cases.

As Figure 5-1 shows, TDD is a cycle so that once you have your failing tests you can begin coding. The idea at this point is to do the bare minimum amount of coding required to make the test pass. In this way, your test *drives* the development of the application. The strictest followers of TDD write code only if a failing test presents the need to do so. However, you can adapt the process to make it work for you. As a baseline, the core features of your application should be driven by the tests that you write. Examples in the chapter illustrate this TDD approach in more detail.

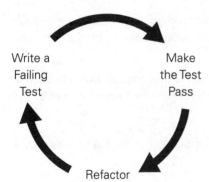

Write a
Failing
Test

Make
the Test
Pass

Refactor

FIGURE 5-1: The test driven development life cycle.

With your tests in place and the code now making them pass, you can enter the next stage, where you have the opportunity to refactor your code. Because in this process, you write the minimum amount of code necessary to get the tests to pass, your code may not even be functional except for passing the test cases. You may need to add more tests to drive the functionality required or be able to refactor the code to be more efficient perhaps. Essentially, you can take some time to make changes that make your code more readable, succinct, and maintainable going forward. You can undertake this process with confidence now that you have tests that pass, because you will know after your refactoring if you have broken any of the newly implemented code. Later down then line, should your application design change or you wish to move some classes around and change the behavior, you can use your test suite to guide you by fixing any failing tests you may create.

Advantages of Test Driven Development

TDD brings many advantages to your project. It ensures that you make testing your aim and part of the actual coding rather than leaving testing to the end, which was the norm in the not too distant past. By making this process your aim, you gain the following:

- As the application evolves, so does the testing suite covering all the functionality of your application.

- Excellent opportunities emerge to engage developers when pair programming, undertaking development practices such as "ping-pong programming," explained later in the chapter.

- Testing tools, such as coverage, ensure that you are testing every part of your application and not leaving any holes in your test suite and keep you on your toes.

- You can have confidence in the code that you have produced because your tests have proved the code behaves in the way the developer expects it to, before going live to production.

- Fail Fast! A full test suite allows you to develop and pick up bugs as they are created, rather than having to find out later in integration testing or worse, production environments in real user scenarios.

- You avoid gold plating. TDD keeps you from adding features and functionality outside of what is required. The cost of a feature is reflected in the effort required to write the tests.

You write the tests for the code that is to be developed, write the code, see the tests pass, and add no more.

Ping-Pong Programming

Ping-pong programming can make pair programming more fun and engaging for the developers involved. With pair programming, the idea is that one person is writing the code while the other is checking the code being written. The pair talk with each other over the design of the code, discuss what they each think is required, and develop the functionality until requirements are met.

What sometimes happens with pair programming, however, is that one member of the pair may be stronger technically than the other. One person may have more experience in the programming language or simply have encountered this development scenario before. This can lead to the more experienced member of the pair taking control of the development process and leaving the less experienced member to watch and perhaps unable to offer any input or advice. This situation, although usually unintentional on any one developer's part, can make pair programming unworkable. This is where ping-pong programming comes in. The concept is simple: One person writes the failing test, and the other writes the code to make it pass. By developing in this way, both developers invest about the same amount of time working with the code and are not watching each other for long periods of time. This engages both developers and allows them to learn from each other while delivering the functionality. The process becomes somewhat of a game, as each developer is effectively creating a challenge for the other to complete. Obviously, this is not supposed to be competitive, though: Both are working toward the same goal. Working in this fashion can accelerate the learning of a developer who would simply have been watching the stronger partner code the problem. If the stronger member of the team writes the test, for example, the less-technical member learns what the code should look like while trying to get the test to pass. As coders develop strength, they can take turns writing the code and the tests.

In my opinion, developing in this way can be hugely beneficial and can be a great process for getting a new starter in your team up to speed on the code base with one of the more senior members of the team.

Test Driving Your Problem

Let's get practical with this now. You should by now have a basic understanding of how you approach TDD, but working through an example in a TDD fashion can really cement the process in your mind.

Here you look at a slightly more complicated example of creating a class that will model a bank account. You obviously need to think of some of the functions that a bank account needs to perform, write the test cases for each function, and then write the code that will make the tests pass. You can then try some refactoring to make your code more readable and reusable.

You could consider that the bank account class would have the following business requirements:

- The customer must be able to uniquely access his bank account and retrieve the balance.
- The customer must be able to deposit funds into her bank account.
- The customer must be able to withdraw funds from his bank account.

These requirements allow you to deliver a minimum viable product at the end of this sprint. If you deliver these requirements, then you have code that can handle the basic responsibilities of a bank account.

74

TESTING PYTHON

Writing Your Failing Test

Imagine you are working in an agile team. At this point, you are free to pick up a story, and the highest priority story would be the first bullet point in the preceding list. You need to be able to uniquely identify the bank account and retrieve its balance. So, following TDD, you must first think about the tests that can be written that will drive the development of this piece of work. What kind of objects and methods do you need to be able to deliver this requirement? You don't have any existing code so far, so perhaps you should start with a test that enables you to create the Account class.

Start with an empty folder for your new project, called Bank. Create a Virtualenv for the project, as described in Chapter 1, also named bank. Add a test directory inside and create a test file named account_test.py.

```
import unittest


class TestAccount(unittest.TestCase):
    def test_account_object_can_be_created(self):
        account = Account()


if __name__ == '__main__':
    unittest.main()
```

This is the most basic test you can write. It will fail because the Account class hasn't been created yet. When you run the test, you are informed that Account is not defined. You must go and create it.

```
$ nosetests
E
======================================================================
ERROR: test_account_object_can_be_created
  (test.account_test.TestAccount)
----------------------------------------------------------------------
Traceback (most recent call last):
  File "/Users/david/workspace/bank/test/account_test.py", line 6,
 in test_account_object_can_be_created
    account = Account()
NameError: global name 'Account' is not defined
```

```
--------------------------------------------------------------

Ran 1 test in 0.010s
FAILED (errors=1)
```

Making Your Test Pass

To make this test pass, you must define the Account class and import it in the test. Outside of the test directory, add a file named account.py and define the class. Again, you code only the most basic functionality to make the test pass.

```
class Account(object):
    pass
```

Add the following import line to the test and run again.

```
from account import Account
```

You should have a passing test now.

```
$ nosetests
.
--------------------------------------------------------------
Ran 1 test in 0.006s
OK
```

Of course, this example is being shown from its most basic level. When you become more comfortable with TDD and Python programming, you can write a lot more of the test before running, then write a lot more of the class. It's all about finding the balance that enables you to drive your development just from tests, without it becoming a tedious process.

Driving More Features with Tests

Now that you have your Account class, you can begin to add some of the functionality specified in the business requirement. You need to be able to uniquely identify a bank account and retrieve its balance. Bank accounts often have an account number to identify them. Add the test that will drive the creation of a constructor for the Account class. The constructor will take an account number and initial balance and stores that information on the object.

```
class TestAccount(unittest.TestCase):
    def test_account_object_returns_current_balance(self):
        account = Account("001", 50)
        self.assertEqual(account.account_number, "001")
        self.assertEqual(account.balance, 50)
```

Running this test will fail in the first instance because the Account class has no constructor and so does not expect the arguments to be passed into it.

```
$ nosetests
E
======================================================================
ERROR: test_account_object_returns_current_balance
(test.account_test.TestAccount)
----------------------------------------------------------------------
Traceback (most recent call last):
  File "/Users/david/workspace/bank/test/account_test.py", line 7,
 in test_account_object_returns_current_balance
    account = Account("001", 50)
TypeError: object() takes no parameters


----------------------------------------------------------------------
Ran 1 test in 0.005s
FAILED (errors=1)
```

The test tells you exactly this, so now the code must be changed to allow the Account class to take these arguments.

```
class Account(object):
    def __init__(self, account_number, balance):
        pass
```

Now when you run the test again, you discover a different error that is due to not storing the values on the object when it is created so that you can access the values later.

```
$ nosetests
E
======================================================================
```

```
ERROR: test_account_object_returns_current_balance
(test.account_test.TestAccount)
------------------------------------------------------------------
Traceback (most recent call last):
  File "/Users/david/workspace/bank/test/account_test.py", line 8,
 in test_account_object_returns_current_balance
    self.assertEqual(account.account_number, 001)
AttributeError: 'Account' object has no attribute 'account_number'


------------------------------------------------------------------
Ran 1 test in 0.006s
FAILED (errors=1)
```

The final change to the Account class assigns the passed in variable to properties. The test can then access these variables through the properties.

```
class Account(object):
    def __init__(self, account_number, balance):
        self.account_number = account_number
        self.balance = balance
```

Now when you run the test, everything passes.

```
$ nosetests
.
------------------------------------------------------------------
Ran 1 test in 0.006s
OK
```

Wrapping Up the Task

The final part of this requirement is to be able to uniquely access the bank account and retrieve the balance. You can create individual Account objects, but they are not stored anywhere in which they can be retrieved easily. It looks like a Bank object is needed to store all the Accounts. The simplest form the Bank object can take is a dictionary, where the key is the account_number and the value is the `balance`.

Create a Bank class that stores the accounts in a dictionary. You need simple methods like add_account and get_account_balance to achieve the functionality. Now that you are getting used to the process of TDD, you can add all the tests you will need and then write the code to make them pass.

Create a test file called bank_test.py in the test directory of the project, with the following tests:

```python
import unittest

from account import Account


class BankTest(unittest.TestCase):
    def test_bank_is_initially_empty(self):
        bank = Bank()
        self.assertEqual({}, bank.accounts)
        self.assertEqual(len(bank.accounts), 0)

    def test_add_account(self):
        bank = Bank()

        account_1 = Account(001, 50)
        account_2 = Account(002, 100)

        bank.add_account(account_1)
        bank.add_account(account_2)

        self.assertEqual(len(bank.accounts), 2)

    def test_get_account_balance(self):
        bank = Bank()

        account_1 = Account(001, 50)

        bank.add_account(account_1)

        self.assertEqual(bank.get_account_balance(001), 50)


if __name__ == '__main__':
    unittest.main()
```

Here you are creating an instance of the Bank class, and in the first test, checking that the accounts dictionary is initialized as empty, creating two accounts, adding them to the bank, and checking that the accounts dictionary does indeed now contain the two items you have added. In the second test, you again create an instance of the Bank class, check that there are no accounts, create an account, and add it to the bank. You then check that the balance for account number 001 is as expected.

You can now run the tests to drive your development. You see what the first failure is and code accordingly.

```
$ nosetests
.EE
==================================================================
ERROR: test_add_account (test.bank_test.BankTest)
------------------------------------------------------------------
Traceback (most recent call last):
  File "/Users/david/workspace/bank/test/bank_test.py", line 6, in
test_add_account
    bank = Bank()
NameError: global name 'Bank' is not defined


==================================================================
ERROR: test_get_account_balance (test.bank_test.BankTest)
------------------------------------------------------------------
Traceback (most recent call last):
  File "/Users/david/workspace/bank/test/bank_test.py", line 19, in
test_get_account_balance
    bank = Bank()
NameError: global name 'Bank' is not defined


------------------------------------------------------------------
Ran 3 tests in 0.009s
FAILED (errors=2)
```

Of course, you have no Bank class. You can go ahead and add this code to the file bank.py as you previously did with the Account class, and add the import statement in the test file.

```
class Bank(object):
    pass
```

Import for test_bank.py:

```
from bank import Bank
```

Running the tests again shows you the next piece of the class that needs to be added:

```
$ nosetests
.EE
======================================================================
ERROR: test_add_account (test.bank_test.BankTest)
----------------------------------------------------------------------
Traceback (most recent call last):
  File "/Users/david/workspace/bank/test/bank_test.py", line 9, in
test_add_account
    self.assertEqual({}, bank.accounts)
AttributeError: 'Bank' object has no attribute 'accounts'


======================================================================
ERROR: test_get_account_balance (test.bank_test.BankTest)
----------------------------------------------------------------------
Traceback (most recent call last):
  File "/Users/david/workspace/bank/test/bank_test.py", line 22, in
test_get_account_balance
    self.assertEqual({}, bank.accounts)
AttributeError: 'Bank' object has no attribute 'accounts'


----------------------------------------------------------------------
Ran 3 tests in 0.009s
FAILED (errors=2)
```

Your test shows that you clearly need to add the accounts attribute that will be the dictionary containing all your accounts. You can add that to the Bank class.

```
class Bank(object):
    def __init__(self):
        self.accounts = {}
```

Running the tests again produces the following results:

```
$ nosetests
.EE
======================================================================
ERROR: test_add_account (test.bank_test.BankTest)
----------------------------------------------------------------------
Traceback (most recent call last):
  File "/Users/david/workspace/bank/test/bank_test.py", line 15,
```

```
in
test_add_account
    bank.add_account(account_1)
AttributeError: 'Bank' object has no attribute 'add_account'


======================================================================
ERROR: test_get_account_balance (test.bank_test.BankTest)
----------------------------------------------------------------------
Traceback (most recent call last):
  File "/Users/david/workspace/bank/test/bank_test.py", line 27,
 in
test_get_account_balance
    bank.add_account(account_1)
AttributeError: 'Bank' object has no attribute 'add_account'


----------------------------------------------------------------------
Ran 3 tests in 0.008s
FAILED (errors=2)
```

Now you are getting to the meat of the application. Clearly the test is indicating that you must code the add_account method. This following code implements this method.

```
    def add_account(self, account):
        self.accounts[account.account_number] = account.balance
```

Running the tests to show where you are shows something like the following.

```
$ nosetests
..E
======================================================================
ERROR: test_get_account_balance (test.bank_test.BankTest)
----------------------------------------------------------------------
Traceback (most recent call last):
  File "/Users/david/workspace/bank/test/bank_test.py", line 29, in
test_get_account_balance
    self.assertEqual(bank.get_account_balance(001), 50)
AttributeError: 'Bank' object has no attribute
  'get_account_balance'


----------------------------------------------------------------------
Ran 3 tests in 0.008s
FAILED (errors=1)
```

Great! The test for `add_account` now passes. You are nearly finished adding all the functionality for this business requirement. As the test suggests, you just need to add the `get_account_balance` method to complete the work on this feature. Add the method shown to the `Bank` class.

```python
def get_account_balance(self, account_number):
    return self.accounts.get(account_number)
```

Then run the tests again to see if you are finished.

```
$ nosetests
...
----------------------------------------------------------------
Ran 3 tests in 0.008s
OK
```

All your tests now pass and the functionality for the business requirement you are coding for has been delivered. Hopefully, this example makes it clear how writing tests first in this way *can* actually drive your coding. With each test failure, it was clear what was required from the class or method to enable the test to pass and therefore meet your requirements. It's worth noting that although this is a relatively simple application, the process scales to any kind of development you are undertaking. As mentioned earlier, you can tailor this process and follow it as strictly as you like. However, at a bare minimum, you should be writing a few tests to ensure that all features are covered by unit tests. Coverage is a great tool (see Chapter 3) for ensuring all your code is covered by tests.

Summary

In this chapter, you were introduced to the flexible development process that is agile. The core concepts of agile development were explained along with why they should be followed, their importance to the process, and the advantages that working in this way can bring to your team. By following the simple pointers offered in "Adapt the Agile Process Now," you can begin using agile on your own personal project or within a development team inside a business. The process is widely adopted and adapted by many top companies in the industry and should you wish to read more about the subject, please consult the resources section.

Following the introduction to agile and how TDD plays its part in the process, you then started to look at practical examples of TDD in action. Ping-pong programming is a great way to engage the developers on your team, especially those who are more used to working on their own. Ping-pong programming is also worthwhile as a learning tool for new team members to get them quickly up to speed, especially when pairing with the more senior and experienced members of the development team.

Wrapping up the chapter, you took an in-depth look at how exactly a piece of functionality within a real application could be test driven to completion. By using the bank account example, you could clearly see how, from the requirements provided, failing tests could be extracted. These failing tests then clearly demonstrated exactly what needed coding to enable the functionality to work and the test to pass. The example also showed how working in this way keeps the developers focused on the problem at hand and delivers only to the exact requirements asked of them.

Resources

The Agile Manifesto: `http://agilemanifesto.org`

NetTuts article on core agile concepts: `http://net.tutsplus.com/articles/general/the-principles-of-agile-development/`

NetTuts article on test driven development (David Sale, your author): `http://net.tutsplus.com/tutorials/python-tutorials/test-driven-development-in-python/`

Chapter 6

Writing Acceptance Tests

IN THIS CHAPTER, you take your testing techniques to the next level. So far, the testing has been focused around the unit level—the individual parts of the application. Now you turn your attention to the full journeys through the code. Does the application actually *behave* as you expect? When you run the application, as the end user will actually use it, do you get the results and output that you expect? If unit testing verifies that the code does exactly what the programmer expects it to do, then acceptance testing verifies that the code does what the user expects it to do.

You will also be shown the development process using acceptance tests. Much in the same way as unit tests allow us to follow the test driven development (TDD) approach, acceptance tests allow the behavior driven development (BDD) approach. You will see how you can apply the process of TDD one step higher and write your acceptance tests first, then your units.

What Is Acceptance Testing?

A relatively new approach to testing, acceptance tests verify the actual behavior of your application and ensure it delivers to the end user exactly what they expect it to. Another aspect that is integral to the agile development process, acceptance testing can be a key structural element in your development cycle, bringing in not just your developers and QA (quality assurance) personnel but also less technical personnel such as business analysts and product owners. These types of tests are often written in plain English (adaptations are available to allow writing in other languages) and so can be read by anyone, to understand exactly what the test is looking to exercise. Underneath these plain text test files are step files, which actually execute the code to perform the test. You see this in action later in the chapter when you work through some acceptance test examples.

Behavior driven development—the process of writing these acceptance tests before writing any code—clearly combines with the TDD approach that you were introduced to in Chapter 5. This leads to the kind of cycle shown in Figure 6-1, where not only do you write the failing unit tests, but you also write a failing acceptance test first.

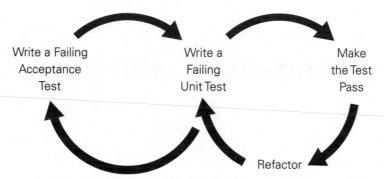

FIGURE 6-1: The development cycle when acceptance testing is added into unit testing.

The process flows something like this:

1. Write failing acceptance tests that cover the expected behavior of the feature you are about to write.

2. Write failing unit tests that cover the functionality that is being developed to allow the acceptance test to pass.

3. Write the code that will make the unit test pass.

4. Refactor the code at this point and check that the unit tests still pass.

5. Ensure your acceptance tests now pass.

6. Your feature is now complete and tested at both the unit and user levels.

One of the plus points of writing acceptance tests as part of your process and not just unit tests is that, as mentioned previously, the acceptance tests are written in plain English. This means that as you write the tests to cover the features you are delivering, you are effectively writing testable documentation for your application. The acceptance tests basically describe the feature and what it should do and so in effect are the documentation of the various features delivered. This format allows business personnel to have a say in how the feature is described. The business can then review the acceptance test feature files and read exactly what the application is delivering.

Anatomy of an Acceptance Test

So far in the chapter, acceptance tests have been described as having an English language "feature" file describing the test and step files that actually execute the code to perform the test. To give you a sense of exactly how the tests will work and be created, this section details exactly what these files are composed of.

One of the most important things to note when writing acceptance tests is that they follow a very familiar style and pattern, regardless of the language they are being implemented in. One of the most famous implementations of acceptance testing comes in the form of "Cucumber" tests, a library written for the Ruby programming language. This library sets the style and tone of acceptance tests and is a format that has been adopted in many languages, including, of course, Python. The implementation for Python is known as "Lettuce," and the framework will be used here to illustrate the anatomy of acceptance tests.

Using Gherkin Syntax

One of the concepts introduced in Cucumber was the definition of the *Gherkin syntax*—a set of keywords that you use to define your acceptance test. The main keywords that make up this syntax are as follows:

- Feature:

- Scenario:

- Scenario Outline:

- Given

- When

- Then

- And

Using these keywords, you can describe your feature in the standard style that Cucumber has defined. So an example Lettuce feature file might look something like this:

```
Feature: Retrieve customer balance
        As a customer of the bank
        I wish to be able to view my current balance

Scenario: Customer retrieves balance successfully
        Given account number 0001 is a valid account
        When I try to retrieve the balance for account number 0001
        Then the balance of the account is "50"
```

The `Feature:` section of the feature file basically describes which aspect of the application this feature is covering. This example is clearly testing retrieval of customers' bank account balances (making use of the example from Chapter 5) and ensures you get the correct result.

The `Scenario:` section is where the test takes place and contains the lines that Lettuce actually executes when you run the test. The test is broken down into the following three parts.

- The `Given` line sets up the account in the application so that you can actually call the code on that account.

- The `When` line actually calls your application with that account and stores the answer.

- The `Then` line performs an assertion that the balance obtained when calling the application for the given account returned the value "50". Essentially this line asserts that the application produces the result you expected.

You may, of course, need more than just the three lines for more complicated tests, in which case you can make use of the `And` keyword to chain multiple `Given/When/Then` statements as required. In such a case, `And` is understood as the same keyword used on the line above it.

The Magic Is in the Step File

The step file connects the feature file's English statements to the Python code that performs the tests. This code comes in the form of a step file, and in the case of Lettuce will look something like the following:

```
from lettuce import *

from bank.account import Account
from bank.bank import Bank


@step(u'account number 0001 is a valid account')
def given_account_number_0001_is_a_valid_account(step):
    account = Account(0001, 50)
    bank = Bank()
    bank.add_account(account)
```

Notice how the step ignores the keyword at the beginning and then uses regular expressions to match the line in the feature file to the step. You then simply name the method something unique and define the behavior of the step in Python code. Because the Lettuce test is executing Python in the background, it makes it much simpler for you to write tests. You don't need to learn anything extra apart from how to import Lettuce and define the step regular expression decorator. This allows you to create highly customizable steps that work for your application, and you can apply good Python practices to make them reusable in many different test cases.

In the preceding example, you could take the account number as a parameter to allow different account numbers to be used for different behavior in your tests. I cover this technique later in the chapter, but it is something worth bearing in mind when coming up with acceptance tests. Especially on a larger project, your steps can quickly become numerous if you don't make them as reusable as possible.

Goals of Acceptance Testing

If you have good unit test coverage, why do you need to spend the effort and time to create a whole set of acceptance tests as well? There is a key distinction between unit tests and acceptance tests. You could consider your unit tests the fundamental foundations on which your application is built. They ensure that the individual elements of your application work as you intend them to, in isolation. Acceptance tests then take these foundations and ensure they work together to support the whole. When you chain your classes and methods together to create a fully functioning application, acceptance tests check that the behavior of your application is as expected. They can also go a step further than just checking responses and their contents. Acceptance tests are classically used for testing web applications, actually clicking around elements of a website as a user would and asserting that the correct items are shown onscreen.

The goals of acceptance testing can be summarized as:

- Ensuring that your application delivers the functionality you expect it to.

- Providing a human-readable description of the functionality under test.

- Incorporating acceptance testing into the agile development process to ensure you have delivered working code and a working application to your specification.

- Providing a regression-testing suite, allowing you to add more functionality and be certain you have not broken or changed the previously delivered behavior.

- Highlighting issues or bugs in your application, as a user would, before it has gone live to your customers.

- Engaging all members of the team in the testing process by allowing even nontechnical personnel to contribute to the description and wording of a feature.

Implementing Developer and QA Collaboration

When teams have dedicated QA personnel, it is easy for the developers to continue just writing their unit tests and leaving things like acceptance testing to the QA members to handle. In practice, it is beneficial for the two parties to sit together and define the failing acceptance tests prior to any code being written. Following this approach allows for writing a good set of tests that cover the full scope of the feature to be delivered. It allows for two different mindsets to think about the problem up front. For example, the QA members may have some ideas of edge cases that the developers have not taken into consideration. By thinking about these problems up front, developers can build in code that will handle such edge cases the first time, rather than having to go back to the code when the QA team discovers edge cases later on. Spending time up front before coding can lead to a much more efficient process and allow developers to deliver their code correctly the first time, meeting all requirements and making the QA person's job much easier.

Letting Behavior Drive Your Problem

You saw the structure of an acceptance earlier in the chapter, but to really cement how you undertake acceptance testing and write tests yourself, you can work through this example using acceptance tests to drive the code being created. Of course, alongside these tests you would also write unit tests (refer to Chapters 2 and 3 for more about unit tests). The main focus in this chapter is the acceptance tests; you can assume that the unit tests have been written for any code you write.

The process you follow here is much the same as the one in the "Test Driving Your Problem" section from Chapter 5. Here you define a story to be played to add some functionality to your bank account application used previously. Let's say you have been presented with the following list of new requirements:

- The customer wishes to view balance information on a web page.

- The customer wants a web page to update the balance.

- The customer wants a web page to make a withdrawal.

The requirements tell you the functionality you need to provide but allow you to make decisions over the technical direction, which is exactly how requirements should be formed in an agile team.

Writing Your Failing Acceptance Test

You are now ready to start work on the first task, which is to allow a customer to view his balance. You could achieve this by allowing the user to enter his account number into a text box and submit the form. The web application would then look up the account and display the balance to the user.

Start by adding your BDD test structure into the previous project. You may want to move your unit tests into a folder called "Unit" under the test directory you created earlier. You can then add a BDD folder alongside that for the Lettuce tests you are about to write. This would give you a structure like this:

```
/bank
    bank/
        *.py files
    templates/
        *.html files
    test/
        unit/
        account_test.py
            bank_test.py
        bdd/
            features/
                bank.feature
            steps/
                steps.py
```

Once you have this structure in place, create a file called `bank.feature` in the location shown previously. Here you are going to write the test description that executes the steps shown earlier in the chapter. Add the following lines to the feature file:

```
Feature: Bank web application to retrieve
        and update customer accounts

        As a customer I wish to be able to view my balance
        and update my balance
        and withdraw from my balance

        Scenario: Retrieve customer balance
        Given I visit the homepage
```

This is the most basic test you can put in place at the moment. It will allow you to drive the creation of the initial web page skeleton from which your application will evolve. If you try to execute this test, it will fail because not only have you not written any code, but you also haven't even implemented the steps for Lettuce to execute! Run the Lettuce command and you will indeed see a prompt and some handy skeleton code to implement your steps.

```
$ lettuce test/bdd/

Feature: Bank web application to retrieve
         and update customer accounts
  # test/bdd/features/bank.feature:1
  As a customer I wish to be able to view my balance
  # test/bdd/features/bank.feature:3
  and update my balance
  # test/bdd/features/bank.feature:4
  and withdraw from my balance
  # test/bdd/features/bank.feature:5

  Scenario: Retrieve customer balance
    # test/bdd/features/bank.feature:7
    Given I visit the homepage
    # test/bdd/features/bank.feature:8

1 feature (0 passed)
1 scenario (0 passed)
1 steps (1 undefined, 0 passed)

You can implement step definitions for undefined
steps with these snippets:

# -*- coding: utf-8 -*-
from lettuce import step

@step(u'I visit the homepage')
def i_visit_the_homepage(step):
    assert False, 'This step must be implemented'
```

The output is fairly lengthy because Lettuce prints the feature file lines along with where they are in the feature file itself. You then see the test statistics (such as number passing/failing) and, of course, the feature is failing because all three steps are undefined. You are then presented with the skeleton steps, and you can now copy and paste the steps into your steps file and add the code to implement the step behavior, as shown next in "Defining Your Steps". The skeleton step definitions can be found towards the bottom of the output and contain the line "This step must be implemented."

Defining Your Steps

Copy the lines from the Lettuce import statement downward and paste them into `steps.py` under the `steps` folder in `bdd`. Because you are testing a web application, you need some way to interact with the web application in the browser. Fortunately, a library called WebTest makes this simple for you. You can also use `nose.tools` from the unit testing framework to use the assertions (such as `assertEqual`) discussed in Chapter 2 under the heading "Useful Methods in Unit Testing".

Before defining the steps, you must first install WebTest using Pip as shown in previous chapters. You can enter the following command at the command line to install WebTest.

```
$ pip install webtest
```

As of the time of writing, the latest version of WebTest was 2.0.15. If you would like to install this specific version, enter the following command instead.

```
$ pip install webtest==2.0.15
```

With WebTest installed, you can now add some code that will check whether you can visit the homepage and get a successful response.

```python
from lettuce import *
from nose.tools import assert_equal
from webtest import TestApp

from bank_app import app


@step(u'I visit the homepage')
def i_visit_the_homepage(step):
    world.browser = TestApp(app)
    world.response = world.browser.get('http://localhost:5000/')
    assert_equal(world.response.status_code, 200)
    assert_equal(world.response.text, u'Hello World!')
```

If you check the imports here, you can see the three libraries are being used as explained. WebTest is vital for you here because it is basically wrapping the Flask (Python web framework) application and starting up an instance in a headless browser for you. This means you don't need to start the server manually but can simply run the Lettuce test as a stand-alone execution. The final import is for your Flask app, which you will create. Finally, the test starts the app in the browser, calling the homepage and then checking the HTTP Status Code is 200 and the response is a simple "Hello World!" message. Note, later in the chapter the application will develop and you will replace the "Hello, World!" text with some other functionality. When you reach such a point, either remove the assertion checking this text or update the test to reflect the new functionality.

Running your test at this stage will fail, of course, and Lettuce informs you where you next need to code.

```
$ lettuce test/bdd/
Traceback (most recent call last):
  File "/Users/username/.virtualenvs/bank/bin/lettuce",
  line 9, in <module>
    load_entry_point('lettuce==0.2.19', 'console_scripts',
    'lettuce')()
  File "/Users/username/.virtualenvs/bank/lib/python2.7/
  site-packages/lettuce/bin.py", line 106, in main
    result = runner.run()
  File "/Users/username/.virtualenvs/bank/lib/python2.7/
  site-packages/lettuce/__init__.py", line 137, in run
    self.loader.find_and_load_step_definitions()
  File "/Users/username/.virtualenvs/bank/lib/python2.7/
  site-packages/lettuce/fs.py", line 49, in
  find_and_load_step_definitions
    module = __import__(to_load)
  File "/Users/username/workspace/bank/test/bdd/steps/steps.py",
  line 4, in <module>
    from bank_app import app
ImportError: cannot import name app
```

Implementing Your Code

If you take a look at the Flask documentation on the website (see the resources at the end of the chapter), the most simple application you can define and allow your test to pass can be coded in about nine lines. Add a file called bank_app.py to the application directory (PROJECT/bank/bank_app.py) of your project and add the following Flask implementation:

```
from flask import Flask
app = Flask(__name__)


@app.route('/')
def hello_world():
    return 'Hello World!'

if __name__ == '__main__':
    app.run()
```

At this point, you can execute the bank_app.py file and Flask's built-in development server starts running locally on your machine on port 5000 by default. To see what the test is seeing, you can start the server and visit http://localhost:5000/ in the browser of your choice. Running the Lettuce test at this point shows that you have now satisfied the first part of your test.

```
$ lettuce test/bdd/

Feature: Bank web application to retrieve
         and update customer accounts
  # test/bdd/features/bank.feature:1
  As a customer I wish to be able to view my balance
  # test/bdd/features/bank.feature:3
  and update my balance
  # test/bdd/features/bank.feature:4
  and withdraw from my balance
  # test/bdd/features/bank.feature:5

  Scenario: Retrieve customer balance
    # test/bdd/features/bank.feature:7
    Given I visit the homepage
    # test/bdd/steps/steps.py:7

1 feature (1 passed)
1 scenario (1 passed)
1 step (1 passed)
```

Developing More of the Feature

You can now start to add in the functional parts of your task. The next step to add to your feature is the ability to submit an account number to search for. To do this, you could write a step that takes in the account number inline and then tries to submit this in the browser.

```
When I enter the account number "1111"
```

You can then capture the number in quotes in the step and use this to form a generic step that will submit any account number you define in a feature file when calling this step. Again, running the Lettuce test provides you with a skeleton to build on to speed up your test development process.

```
@step(u'I enter the account number "([^"]*)"')
def when_i_enter_the_account_number_group1(step, account_number):
```

```
form = world.response.forms['account-form']
form['account_number'] = account_number
world.form_response = form.submit()
assert_equal(world.form_response.status_code, 200)
```

This step is basically checking for the existence of the form and getting hold of that as an object the user can then "fill out." You set the account number to match the one passed into the step. The step then submits the form and checks that the response is okay. Executing this test shows you that a form with the ID of `"account-form"` must be created on the web page. You can then go ahead and add the code for that:

```
Traceback (most recent call last):
  File "/Users/username/.virtualenvs/bank/lib/python2.7/
  site-packages/lettuce/core.py", line 144, in __call__
    ret = self.function(self.step, *args, **kw)
  File
"/Users/username/workspace/bank/test/bdd/steps/steps.py",
  line 14, in when_i_enter_the_account_number_group1
    form = world.response.forms['account-form']
  KeyError: 'account-form'

1 feature (0 passed)
1 scenario (0 passed)
2 steps (1 failed, 1 passed)
```

Because you now need to add more than just text to the web page, it is a good point to set up a Flask template. To do this, you simply add a `"templates"` directory at the same level in which the Flask app is created—in this case, the root level of your project. Add a file called `index.html` within this folder. You can then make use of the Flask `render_template` function to return the HTML page you create in the templates as your response for the root of the web application.

bank_app.py

The page is the entry point to your application, defining the routes of your web app. Here, you are defining that when you hit the route of the web application, "/", you serve the `index.html` template file.

```
from flask import Flask, render_template
app = Flask(__name__)

@app.route('/')
def hello_world():
    return render_template ('index.html')
```

index.html

This main HTML page for your web application is served by the root of the application. This HTML takes the form of a Python Jinja 2 template, which allows for Python variables and code to be injected and interpreted at runtime to produce a web page with dynamic content.

```html
<!DOCTYPE html>
<html>
<head>
    <title>Bank App</title>
</head>
<body>

<form id="account form">
    <label>Acount Number: </label><input name="account_number"
    type="text"/>
    <input type="submit"/>
</form>

</body>
</html>
```

The Lettuce test will pass at this point and you can then move on to actually making use of the account number to retrieve the current balance and display it to the user.

```
$ lettuce test/bdd/

Feature: Bank web application to retrieve and update customer
  accounts # test/bdd/features/bank.feature:1
  As a customer I wish to be able to view my balance
  # test/bdd/features/bank.feature:3
  and update my balance
  # test/bdd/features/bank.feature:4
  and withdraw from my balance
  # test/bdd/features/bank.feature:5

  Scenario: Retrieve customer balance
  # test/bdd/features/bank.feature:7
    Given I visit the homepage
  # test/bdd/steps/steps.py:7
    When I enter the account number "1111"
  # test/bdd/steps/steps.py:13
```

```
1 feature (1 passed)
1 scenario (1 passed)
2 steps (2 passed)
```

Should you find any problems or failures in your tests or running your Flask application, you can make use of Flask's great built-in debug option. Earlier in this chapter, you added code to execute the `app.run()` method when you execute the `bank_app.py` file. This starts up the Flask development server, so that you can try visiting your application in your local web browser. By default, Flask's debug option is set to False. Meaning when a problem occurs in your code, you are simply shown an "Internal Server" error message by your browser. If you add the `debug=True` option to the `app.run()` method, you can get a highlighted stack trace showing you the problem in the code directly. Your code in the `bank_app.py` file changes like so to add the debug option.

```
if __name__ == '__main__':
    app.run(debug=True)
```

Delivering the Finished Article

Add the final step, which will check that the current balance displays as expected. This will take the balance in the step definition and then assert that the balance shown in the browser is the same as that passed into the step. Again, make use of the skeleton generated to give you the starting point.

```
Then I see a balance of "50"
```

Add the step definition to perform the check.

```
...
from nose.tools import assert_equal, assert_in
from lettuce import *
...

@step(u'I see a balance of "([^"]*)"')
def then_i_see_a_balance_of_group1(step, expected_balance):
    assert_in ("Balance: {}".format(expected_balance),
 world.form_response.text)
```

Executing the test allows you to see the failure and write the code to make this Lettuce test pass and complete the feature.

```
$ lettuce test/bdd/
...
    Traceback (most recent call last):
      File "/Users/username/.virtualenvs/bank/lib/python2.7/
      site-packages/lettuce/core.py", line 144, in __call__
        ret = self.function(self.step, *args, **kw)
      File "/Users/username/workspace/bank/test/bdd/steps/steps.py",
      line 21, in then_i_see_a_balance_of_group1
        assert_in("Balance: {}".format(expected_balance),
        world.form_response.text)
      File "/usr/local/Cellar/python/2.7.5/
            Frameworks/Python.framework/
            Versions/2.7/lib/python2.7/
            unittest/case.py", line 805, in assertIn
        self.fail(self._formatMessage(msg, standardMsg))
      File "/usr/local/Cellar/python/2.7.5/
            Frameworks/Python.framework/Versions/2.7/
            lib/python2.7/unittest/case.py", line 412,
            in fail
        raise self.failureException(msg)
    AssertionError: 'Balance: 50' not found
    in u'<!DOCTYPE html>\n<html>\n<head>\n
        <title>Bank    App</title>\n</head>\n<body>\n\n
        <form id="account-form">\n
        <label>Acocunt Number: </label>\n
        <input name="account_number" type="text"/>\n
        <input type="submit"/>\n</form>\n\n</body>\n</html>'

1 feature (0 passed)
1 scenario (0 passed)
3 steps (1 failed, 2 passed)
```

The test clearly shows that `Balance:  50` is not being displayed on the page. When you submit the form, it basically calls the homepage again with a GET parameter in the URL of `"/?account_number=NUMBER"`. Flask can grab this parameter and make a call to your Bank class to obtain the data you need. This can then be passed to the template and rendered appropriately.

Obtain the value being submitted as a GET parameter in the `bank_app.py` code.

```
from flask import Flask, render_template, request
```

```
from bank.bank import Bank
app = Flask(__name__)
BANK = Bank()


@app.route('/')
def hello_world():
    account_number = request.args.get('account_number')
    balance = BANK.get_account_balance(account_number)
    return render_template('index.html', balance=balance)

if __name__ == '__main__':
    app.run(debug=True)
```

Notice how the Bank class has been made a singleton so that you can access it from within your test. You need this to add test accounts that you can retrieve later. Flask exposes the request to you, so this can be leveraged to obtain the arguments that are passed in. You can then retrieve the balance data and pass it to the template as a keyword argument to be displayed in the template.

```html
<!DOCTYPE html>
<html>
<head>
    <title>Bank App</title>
</head>
<body>

<form id="account-form">
    <label>Acocunt Number: </label><input name="account_number"
    type="text"/>
    <input type="submit"/>
</form>

{% if balance %}
Balance: {{ balance }}
{% endif %}

</body>
</html>
```

Now the test will fail, because you do not have any accounts stored in the bank. Therefore, one final step must be added—effectively, a setup step that would occur in a unit test, for example, to place the account data into the bank like it would be for the real application. Your scenario in the feature file becomes:

```
Scenario: Retrieve customer balance
Given I create account "1111" with balance of "50"
And I visit the homepage
When I enter the account number "1111"
Then I see a balance of "50"
```

And the code to allow the step to define the account would be something like this:

```
...
from bank.account import Account
from bank_app import app, BANK
...
@step(u'I create account "([^"]*)" with balance of "([^"]*)"')
def i_create_account_with_balance_of_group1(step, account_number,
                                            balance):
    a = Account(account_number, balance)
    BANK.add_account(a)
```

Now when you execute the test you see all steps are passing and you have successfully delivered your first feature in a behavior driven fashion.

```
$ lettuce test/bdd/
Feature: Bank web application to retrieve
         and update customer accounts
  # test/bdd/features/bank.feature:1
  As a customer I wish to be able to view my balance
  # test/bdd/features/bank.feature:3
  and update my balance
  # test/bdd/features/bank.feature:4
  and withdraw from my balance
  # test/bdd/features/bank.feature:5

  Scenario: Retrieve customer balance
    # test/bdd/features/bank.feature:7
    Given I create account "1111" with balance of "50"
    # test/bdd/steps/steps.py:8
    And I visit the homepage
    # test/bdd/steps/steps.py:13
    When I enter the account number "1111"
```

```
    # test/bdd/steps/steps.py:19
    Then I see a balance of "50"
    # test/bdd/steps/steps.py:26
1 feature (1 passed)
1 scenario (1 passed)
4 steps (4 passed)
```

Advanced Acceptance Test Techniques

In the example used to show the BDD process, you made use of just the standard set of key words and single line steps in the feature file. However, you can use more advanced techniques within your feature to achieve processes such as running a test with multiple different sets of data. You can also provide tables to steps to pass in larger data sets than just a few variables in the step definition. This section of the chapter gives you an idea of how to use such features, so that you can create the most useful, efficient, and reusable acceptance tests for your application.

Scenario Outline

When you want to process the same test with different values, rather than define the test each time with the new data you can write one single test that essentially loops over your data set and passes in those values to your test. To illustrate such an example, you can imagine that when retrieving balances you need to be able to obtain the balance for any account defined. You should be able to change the test that checks that account "1111" has a balance of "50" to allow a multitude of different accounts and balances to be checked.

```
Feature: Bank web application to retrieve and update customer
  accounts
    As a customer I wish to be able to view my balance
    and update my balance
    and withdraw from my balance

    Scenario Outline: Retrieve customer balance
      Given I create account "<account_number>"
      with balance of "<balance>"
      And I visit the homepage
      When I enter the account number "<account_number>"
      Then I see a balance of "<balance>"
```

```
Examples:
  |account_number|balance|
  |1111          |50     |
  |2222          |100    |
  |3333          |500    |
  |4444          |1000   |
```

Notice how the scenario does not need to change much, essentially replacing values for variables and providing a table of data for the scenario to process through. The step definition remains exactly as it was; you simply put the variables in the quotes and the step is able to execute as it did with the hardcoded values of 1111 and 50.

Tables of Data in Scenarios

In a similar fashion to the scenario outlines, you can actually pass in a table of data into a step definition. This is useful for occasions where you need to check lots of data, such as in a JSON response. Like the preceding scenario outlines example, you create your table using the | ("pipe") symbol and giving each column a title to describe the values in it. To illustrate this technique, you can rewrite the step in the example "Given I create account" to expect a table of account numbers and balances rather than inline as you have been doing.

```
Feature: Bank web application to retrieve and update customer
  accounts

    As a customer I wish to be able to view my balance
    and update my balance
    and withdraw from my balance

    Scenario Outline: Retrieve customer balance
      Given I create the following account:
          |account_number|balance|
          |1111          |50     |
      And I visit the homepage
      When I enter the account number "1111"
      Then I see a balance of "50"
```

Of course, you now need to create a step definition for this table style step, and if you run the tests it will produce the skeleton step definition for you to expand upon.

```
@step(u'I create the following account:')
def i_create_the_following_account(step):
    for row in step.hashes:
        a = Account(row['account_number'], row['balance'])
        BANK.add_account(a)
```

The step essentially is using the same code as earlier, except now you process each row in the table, allowing the creation of multiple accounts in one step. You access the table using the `step.hashes` call that Lettuce provides to expose the data passed in. Each `row` in the hashes is essentially a Python `dict` object, allowing you to access the data by the column title defined in the table.

Summary

Putting it simply, acceptance testing is as much a vital part of testing as unit tests. Unit tests form a firm foundation for your application, ensuring the building blocks work as you expect in isolation. Acceptance tests check that your application works in the way the user will expect it to. By writing tests such as these, you are adding yet another layer of protection for your application before it goes live to the public in any form. Doing so allows you to find and debug problems that may arise in the code before those problems reach a production environment where their impact could cause loss of money or reputation to your business or project.

In this chapter, you covered the exact structure of an acceptance test in the Python library Lettuce. You were introduced to feature and step files that enable you to define the test and ensure that it checks the behavior of your application as you define it.

Other areas of the chapter explained the kind of collaboration this style of testing can bring between people such as your developers and QA personnel to create the best possible test cases for your application scenarios. This also ensures clarity across a team, making sure that team members understand what is to be built and what is being worked toward.

Advantages of this process were discussed, offering a view on why you should put the time and effort into creating an acceptance test suite alongside your unit tests. You were also shown how this fits into the agile development process, and by baking your testing into the development cycle, you can build up a comprehensive tests suite without the pain of trying to implement such tests later.

Finally, you were given a full walk-through of developing in a BDD manner and shown how acceptance tests can drive the development of your application's features. By leveraging Lettuce testing with WebTest, you can ensure web applications are tested as the user expects to see them in the browser.

Resources

Flask Web Framework: `http://flask.pocoo.org`

Lettuce BDD Testing Framework: `http://lettuce.it`

WebTest Browser testing library: `http://webtest.pythonpaste.org/en/latest/`

Chapter 7
Utilizing Acceptance Test Tools

IN THIS CHAPTER you will strengthen your acceptance testing practices by learning about some of the tools available and the features they offer. Leveraging these tools, you can make your development cycle easier and more efficient, enabling you to automate some of the things you need to do every day, such as running your entire test suite as part of a build process. In this chapter, you look at the Cucumber package, which is a Ruby package that sets the standard for acceptance testing in this way. You take a more in-depth look at the Lettuce library introduced in Chapter 6 alongside some options and features it offers apart from the standard test execution.

The Robot test framework offers an alternative approach to this style of testing, and you compare its design and feature set with the testing shown so far. Having some knowledge about a few test tools can help you decide which is best for your development situation Whatever acceptance testing framework you chose, the ideology behind testing in this way can bring great benefits in terms of assurance and quality around your deliverables.

Cucumber: The Acceptance Test Standard

Chapter 6 introduced you to acceptance testing and behavior driven development (BDD). It's fair to say that the Ruby community and, in particular, the Cucumber tool that arose from that community have had a huge say in defining how this testing should be done. To a great extent, the Ruby community has placed a focus on testing. Python follows the Ruby community's lead by placing a focus on testing, as evidenced by the Lettuce library, which now shares many features offered by the Cucumber library. Cucumber defined the style of writing the business definition of a "feature" in your own language and being able to execute that feature as a way of testing your application.

The Cucumber development team offers a great website of content centered on its whole philosophy behind this style of testing. I recommend the site as background reading to anyone wanting true understanding of BDD testing in this way. You can find the site at `http://cukes.info`.

Lettuce in Detail

Now that you understand the basics of Lettuce testing in Python and the features and ideas it has ported from the Cucumber library, it is worth looking into Lettuce as a testing tool. Lettuce supports many useful features as a test runner. Having these features in your testing arsenal can help you build an effective, maintainable BDD testing suite alongside the unit testing suite you built earlier in the book.

Tagging

Tags are a key feature of Lettuce and other BDD style testing tools. It is also a feature provided by the nosetest runner, which uses a very similar style to Lettuce tags. Using tags as part of your development process enables your QA team members and developers to work together seamlessly. Tags let you check in tests that currently fail to prevent them from running as part of your build. Using tags in this way QA testers can write Lettuce tests and check them in before developers are ready to work on them. The developer then simply removes the tag from the test when he or she has made it pass.

Another useful process tags enable is the capability to run selected tests easily. Say you are working on some feature and you run your build to see if all the tests are still passing. You find that one or two acceptance tests are failing because of some change you have made. You can quickly tag those tests and run just those in isolation while you debug and fix the code to make them pass. You can then simply remove the tags and run your full build as normal before checking in. Tagging is a simple act that makes your everyday development process much easier.

How do you implement tags with Lettuce? The process is simple and makes use of decorators above your scenario definitions in the feature file. You then pass the value used into the `--tags` argument and Lettuce will search for scenarios that have that tag. Here's an example:

```
Feature: Bank web application to retrieve and update customer
  accounts

  As a customer I wish to be able to view my balance
  and update my balance
  and withdraw from my balance
```

```
Scenario: Retrieve customer balance
  Given I create the following account:
    | account_number | balance |
    | 1111           | 50      |
  And I visit the homepage
  When I enter the account number "1111"
  Then I see a balance of "50"

Scenario: Retrieve some other account
  Given I create the following account:
    | account_number | balance |
    | 2222           | 100     |
  And I visit the homepage
  When I enter the account number "2222"
  Then I see a balance of "100"
```

Here you are using the example from Chapter 6 with an extra scenario defined. Now when you run this in the normal way, Lettuce executes both scenarios.

```
$ lettuce test/bdd/

Feature: Bank web application to retrieve and update customer
accounts
  # test/bdd/features/bank.feature:1
  As a customer I wish to be able to view my balance
  # test/bdd/features/bank.feature:3
  and update my balance
  # test/bdd/features/bank.feature:4
  and withdraw from my balance
  # test/bdd/features/bank.feature:5

  Scenario: Retrieve customer balance
  # test/bdd/features/bank.feature:7
    Given I create the following account:
  # test/bdd/steps/steps.py:13
      | account_number | balance |
      | 1111           | 50      |
    And I visit the homepage
    # test/bdd/steps/steps.py:19
    When I enter the account number "1111"
    # test/bdd/steps/steps.py:25
```

```
      Then I see a balance of "50"
      # test/bdd/steps/steps.py:32

  Scenario: Retrieve some other account
    # test/bdd/features/bank.feature:15
    Given I create the following account:
      # test/bdd/steps/steps.py:13
      | account_number | balance |
      | 2222           | 100     |
    And I visit the homepage
    # test/bdd/steps/steps.py:19
    When I enter the account number "2222"
    # test/bdd/steps/steps.py:25
    Then I see a balance of "100"
    # test/bdd/steps/steps.py:32

1 feature (1 passed)
2 scenarios (2 passed)
8 steps (8 passed)
```

Now what if you had a problem with the second scenario and wanted to execute just that one in isolation? Add the tag above the scenario.

```
  ...
  @mytag
  Scenario: Retrieve some other account
    Given I create the following account:
      | account_number | balance |
      | 2222           | 100     |
    And I visit the homepage
    When I enter the account number "2222"
    Then I see a balance of "100"
```

Running the command produces the output shown.

```
$ lettuce --tag=mytag test/bdd/

Feature: Bank web application to retrieve
and update customer accounts
  # test/bdd/features/bank.feature:1
  As a customer I wish to be able to view my balance
  # test/bdd/features/bank.feature:3
  and update my balance
```

```
# test/bdd/features/bank.feature:4
and withdraw from my balance
# test/bdd/features/bank.feature:5

@mytag
Scenario: Retrieve some other account
  # test/bdd/features/bank.feature:16
  Given I create the following account:
  # test/bdd/steps/steps.py:13
    | account_number | balance |
    | 2222           | 100     |
  And I visit the homepage
  # test/bdd/steps/steps.py:19
  When I enter the account number "2222"
  # test/bdd/steps/steps.py:25
  Then I see a balance of "100"
  # test/bdd/steps/steps.py:32

1 feature (1 passed)
1 scenario (1 passed)
4 steps (4 passed)
```

Clearly, when you add the tag to the scenario and the `--tag` option to the Lettuce test runner, it executes only the tests which you have provided the tag for. You can now tag as needed and make this a part of your everyday development cycle. It is worth noting the tag can be any string you like. You should come up with some standard for marking tests that are waiting on development work , such as `@pending`. This way, you can set up your build process to ignore any tests that have such a tag so that they don't cause your build to fail. You can ignore tags by placing a minus sign (-) in front of the tag in the `--tag` option. If you run the following code, the scenario with account 1111 executed rather than account 2222, as in the preceding example.

```
$ lettuce --tag=-mytag test/bdd/

Feature: Bank web application to retrieve
and update customer accounts
  # test/bdd/features/bank.feature:1
  As a customer I wish to be able to view my balance
  # test/bdd/features/bank.feature:3
  and update my balance
  # test/bdd/features/bank.feature:4
  and withdraw from my balance
  # test/bdd/features/bank.feature:5
```

```
Scenario: Retrieve customer balance
  # test/bdd/features/bank.feature:7
  Given I create the following account:
  # test/bdd/steps/steps.py:13
    | account_number | balance |
    | 1111           | 50      |
  And I visit the homepage
  # test/bdd/steps/steps.py:19
  When I enter the account number "1111"
  # test/bdd/steps/steps.py:25
  Then I see a balance of "50"
  # test/bdd/steps/steps.py:32

1 feature (1 passed)
1 scenario (1 passed)
4 steps (4 passed)
```

Fail Fast

When running your Lettuce tests as part of your build, you may want to know about failures straightaway. Unless you want to see the entire status of your test suite, you can set Lettuce to stop execution of your tests when it encounters its first failing test. This can also be useful locally on your development machine, where you can fail your build sooner and have a quicker feedback loop to alert you to the need for additional changes. The fail fast feature is again enabled by the use of a command-line option when running the Lettuce tests.

```
$ lettuce --failfast test/bdd/

Feature: Bank web application to retrieve
and update customer accounts
  # test/bdd/features/bank.feature:1
  As a customer I wish to be able to view my balance
  # test/bdd/features/bank.feature:3
  and update my balance
  # test/bdd/features/bank.feature:4
  and withdraw from my balance
  # test/bdd/features/bank.feature:5

  Scenario: Retrieve customer balance
    # test/bdd/features/bank.feature:7
```

```
Given I create the following account:
# test/bdd/steps/steps.py:13
  | account_number | balance |
  | 1111           | 50      |
And I visit the homepage
# test/bdd/steps/steps.py:19
When I enter the account number "1111"
# test/bdd/steps/steps.py:25
Then I see a balance of "100"
# test/bdd/steps/steps.py:32
Traceback (most recent call last):
  File "/Users/username/.virtualenvs/bank/lib/python2.7/
  site-packages/lettuce/core.py", line 144, in __call__
    ret = self.function(self.step, *args, **kw)
  File "/Users/username/workspace/bank/test/bdd/steps/steps.py",
  line 33, in i_see_a_balance_of_group1
    assert_in("Balance: {}".format(expected_balance),
    world.form_response.text)
  File
"/usr/local/Cellar/python/2.7.5/Frameworks/Python.framework/
Versions/2.7/lib/python2.7/unittest/case.py", line 805,
in assertIn
    self.fail(self._formatMessage(msg, standardMsg))
  File
"/usr/local/Cellar/python/2.7.5/Frameworks/Python.framework/
Versions/2.7/lib/python2.7/unittest/case.py", line 412,
in fail
    raise self.failureException(msg)
  AssertionError: 'Balance: 100' not found in
  u'<!DOCTYPE html>\n<html>\n<head>\n      <title>Bank
  App</title>\n</head>\n<body>\n\n<form id="account-form">\n
  <label>Account Number: </label><input name="account_number"
  type="text"/>\n      <input type="submit"/>\n</form>\n\n\n\n
  Balance: 50\n\n\n\n</body>\n</html>'

Lettuce aborted running any more tests because was called
with the '--failfast' option

0 feature (0 passed)
0 scenario (0 passed)
0 step (0 passed)
```

Passing the –failfast argument to the Lettuce test runner will stop the test as expected on the first failure. Here a change has been made to the first test to expect a balance of 100 instead of 50. By causing this test to fail and using the fail fast option, the test runner stopped at this point, showing 0 features or scenarios were fully executed. Lettuce also informs you that it was the option you passed in that caused it to stop at this point.

Nosetest Integration

Unfortunately, the Python community hasn't developed much in the way of tooling between Nosetest and Lettuce. However, one package of note enables you to run your Lettuce and unit tests together using Nosetest, which is useful for creating a build process for running your tests. The package is called nose-lettuce and essentially provides a --with-lettuce option to the Nosetest runner, among other options, to enable you to execute your Lettuce tests before your unit tests.

Using the example bank project, try out this plug-in. The author of the nose-lettuce package has chosen not to release this to PyPi at the time of writing and so it must be installed from GitHub, like so:

```
$ pip install https://github.com/passy/nose-lettuce/tarball/master
```

Once you have installed it, you can issue the following command to execute the set of Lettuce tests alongside the unit tests that are within the project:

```
$ nosetests --with-lettuce --lettuce-path=test/bdd/ -s test/unit/

Feature: Bank web application to retrieve
and update customer accounts
  # test/bdd/features/bank.feature:1
  As a customer I wish to be able to view my balance
  # test/bdd/features/bank.feature:3
  and update my balance
  # test/bdd/features/bank.feature:4
  and withdraw from my balance
  # test/bdd/features/bank.feature:5

  Scenario: Retrieve customer balance
    # test/bdd/features/bank.feature:7
    Given I create the following account:
    # test/bdd/steps/steps.py:13
      | account_number | balance |
      | 1111           | 50      |
    And I visit the homepage
    # test/bdd/steps/steps.py:19
```

```
    When I enter the account number "1111"
    # test/bdd/steps/steps.py:25
    Then I see a balance of "50"
    # test/bdd/steps/steps.py:32

  @mytag
  Scenario: Retrieve some other account
    # test/bdd/features/bank.feature:16
    Given I create the following account:
    # test/bdd/steps/steps.py:13
      | account_number | balance |
      | 2222           | 100     |
    And I visit the homepage
    # test/bdd/steps/steps.py:19
    When I enter the account number "2222"
    # test/bdd/steps/steps.py:25
    Then I see a balance of "100"
    # test/bdd/steps/steps.py:32

1 feature (1 passed)
2 scenarios (2 passed)
8 steps (8 passed)
...


----------------------------------------------------------------
Ran 3 tests in 0.001s
OK
```

Using this plug-in enables you to take advantage of some of the tooling around Nosetests, such as coverage reports, and build the Lettuce tests into that process. More documentation and information can be found at the GitHub page: `https://github.com/passy/nose-lettuce`. Do try to contribute or submit issues to the author to encourage more development to make this an even more useful tool for the Python and BDD communities.

Robot: An Alternative Test Framework

Robot is a Python library that provides a slightly different format to the acceptance testing tools you have seen so far. Developed by Nokia under an open source license, the library has seen active development since its release. As of December 3, 2013, it is at version 2.8.3.

I found through using it that the library has some fairly decent support and tooling. The package has great support in continuous integration tool Jenkins, for example, with plug-ins providing test results output, tracking the amount of tests, and highlighting failing tests.

Robot tests follow some of the structure philosophies that Lettuce demonstrates, such as having a readable feature file and step definitions that execute the code to perform the test. Robot makes use of spacing and a tabular format to parse the feature file; in that respect, Robot is stricter in its style for producing these kinds of tests.

Again, because Robot makes use of Python "under the hood," you can use WebTest to drive some of the interaction with the application and make sending requests and parsing responses easy. In the next section, I convert the Lettuce test from Chapter 6 to a Robot test case. Some of the subtle differences between the two libraries' approaches will be explained along the way.

Installing Robot

Installing the Robot framework is a simple process similar to most other libraries covered in this book. You essentially use Python's "Pip" package manager to install the library and then call the included test runner from the command line. As of February 2014, the current version of Robot framework is 2.8.4; if you'd like to use that version, ensure you add ==2.8.4 during installation.

To install the Robot framework, execute the following code:

```
$ pip install robotframework==2.8.4
```

Alternatively, add the following code to your `requirements.txt` file as shown:

```
robotframework==2.8.4
```

Then run this command.

```
$ pip install -r requirements.txt
```

Writing a Test Case

Equivalent to the feature file from Lettuce, test cases are human-readable documentation stating the intent of the test. The test case is made up of what Robot calls "keywords," and they form the syntax of your test case file. These files are typically just in the text file format (`.txt`), and that allows you to create and edit them in any editor you choose. The keywords can be provided as standard by the Robot framework, or a Robot library you either have imported or written yourself. This example makes use of a custom-built library of keywords so that you can use the WebTest library. The official Robot website (`http://robotframe work.org`) has plenty of documentation for you to read.

To begin, convert your Lettuce feature file from Chapter 6 to a Robot test case and see how it looks. Call the file `bank.txt` and place it in the directory `test/bdd/robot/tests`.

```
*** Settings ***
Documentation      Example Robot tests for
...                Bank application

Resource           ../steps/resource.txt
Resource           ../steps/steps.txt



*** Test Cases ***
Retrieve customer balance
    Given I create the account 1111 with balance 50
    When I retrieve the account 1111
    And the balance should be 50
```

Inspect the code from the first line downward to learn the different sections the test case deals with. The `Settings` section allows you to place some explanatory text for the test case and to give the user some background. Note the use of the triple dots to allow for line continuation of the `Documentation` string. Next up, the keywords are imported from files in the project so that you can call them in test cases. Following the `Settings` section are the actual test cases themselves. Notice how similar they are to the Lettuce feature file, providing an easily readable explanation of what this feature of your application is supposed to be doing.

Implementing Keywords

Of course, as before, this test case won't do anything without the supporting keywords underneath. The two files that you see imported as `Resources` will show the two ways in which you can map code to the line in the test case.

```
*** Settings ***
Documentation      A resource file with reusable variables.

Library            robotLibrary.py

*** Variables ***
${SERVER}          localhost:5000
```

The preceding is the `resource.txt` file (which should be placed in the directory `test/bdd/robot/steps`) and is a very handy file to set up the imports of your steps in your test cases. It allows you to add your own library, such as the `robotLibrary.py` (placed in the same directory) and to bring in third-party libraries, which extend the keywords available. It also provides the capability to set global variables that will be available to any test cases in which you include this file. For instance, if you need to call the same URL for your server in many test cases, you can define the `${SERVER}` variable here in just the one place. This will make it easier to maintain your test cases should the URL change in the future.

```python
from nose.tools import assert_equal, assert_in
from webtest import TestApp

from bank.bank_app import app, BANK
from bank.account import Account

class robotLibrary(object):

    def __init__(self):
        self.browser = None
        self.response = None
        self.form_response = None

    def Create_Account(self, account_number, balance):
        a = Account(account_number, balance)
        BANK.add_account(a)

    def Visit_Homepage(self):
        self.browser = TestApp(app)
        self.response = self.browser.get('http://localhost:5000/')
        assert_equal(self.response.status_code, 200)

    def Enter_Account(self, account_number):
        form = self.response.forms['account-form']
        form['account_number'] = account_number
        self.form_response = form.submit()
        assert_equal(self.form_response.status_code, 200)

    def Get_Balance(self, expected_balance):
        assert_in("Balance: {}".format(expected_balance),
    self.form_response.text)
```

The next file of interest is `robotLibrary.py`. In this file, you can essentially write any Python code that is required and then call them as keywords in your step definitions. The two things of note here are, first, that the code used is almost identical to the step definitions used for Lettuce, aside from the need to store values on the class rather than in the Lettuce `world` object. Secondly, the syntax used to allow these methods to be called as keywords. The method name essentially becomes the keyword without the underscore, so `Create_Account` becomes `Create Account` when used in the step definitions and test cases. That brings you to the final piece of the puzzle, which is the `steps.txt` file. This is the direct mapping between the test case and any code underneath.

```
*** Settings ***
Documentation      Step definitions

*** Variables ***
${HOME URL}         ''

*** Keywords ***
I create the account ${account_number} with balance ${balance}
    Create Account      ${account_number}      ${balance}

I retrieve the account ${account_number}
    Visit Homepage
    Enter Account       ${account_number}

the balance should be ${balance}
    Get Balance         ${balance}
```

Notably, the steps file is similar to the test case file, especially at the start, with the same settings and documentation setup. The file instructs Robot on what it is defining using the starred sections. At this point, it becomes clear that these are the keyword mappings to the test case file shown earlier. Because the `resource.txt` file is being loaded in the test case alongside this `steps.txt` case, the keywords defined in the Python code `robotLibrary.py` are available to these step definitions. As such, you can call Create Account and the others as necessary for the test case. The use of `${}` enables you to specify and capture variables that are in the test case lines. You can then pass these through to the methods and use them in the Python code as expected.

Running Robot Tests

Everything is now in place for you to test your application using these Robot test cases and supporting files. To execute the test, you simply need to run the `pybot` command on the command line that is provided by the library upon installation. You also need to pass the location of your Robot tests to the command for it to be able to execute them. With a project structure such as the one you have created, like so...

```
/$PROJECT (Your directory name to hold the project files)
    /bank
        __init__.py
        account.py
        bank.py
        bank_app.py
        /templates
    /test
        __init__.py
        /robot
            /tests
                bank.txt
            /steps
                resource.txt
                robotLibrary.py
                steps.py
```

. . . you would execute your Robot tests, like so:

```
$ pybot test/robot/
==================================================================
Robot
==================================================================
Robot.Tests
==================================================================
Robot.Tests.Bank :: Example Robot tests for\nBank application
==================================================================
Retrieve customer balance
| PASS |
------------------------------------------------------------------
Robot.Tests.Bank :: Example Robot tests for
| PASS |
1 critical test, 1 passed, 0 failed
1 test total, 1 passed, 0 failed
==================================================================
Robot.Tests                                              | PASS |
1 critical test, 1 passed, 0 failed
1 test total, 1 passed, 0 failed
==================================================================
Robot                                                    | PASS |
1 critical test, 1 passed, 0 failed
1 test total, 1 passed, 0 failed
==================================================================
```

```
Output:   /Users/username/workspace/bank/output.xml
Log:      /Users/username/workspace/bank/log.html
Report:   /Users/username/workspace/bank/report.html
```

The output from Robot is really quite nice and provides a clear breakdown of exactly where and what it is executing. It shows which test cases are passing and gives you a breakdown of how many passed or failed. If you purposefully break the test, you can get an idea of how test failures would be communicated to you. In the following case bank.txt is altered to expect 1000 in account 1111.

```
...
Retrieve customer balance
    Given I create the account 1111 with balance 50
    When I retrieve the account 1111
    And the balance should be 1000
```

Robot now reports a failure.

```
$ pybot test/robot/
==================================================================
Robot
==================================================================
Robot.Tests
==================================================================
Robot.Tests.Bank :: Example Robot tests for\nBank application
==================================================================
Retrieve customer balance                                | FAIL |
'Balance: 1000' not found in u'<!DOCTYPE html>\n<html>\n<head>\n
<title>Bank App</title>\n</head>\n<body>\n\n<form id=
"account-form">\n
<label>Account Number: </label><input name="account_number"
 type="text"/>\n
<input type="submit"/>\n</form>\n\n\n\nBalance:
50\n\n\n\n</body>\n</html>'
------------------------------------------------------------------
Robot.Tests.Bank :: Example Robot tests for             | FAIL |
1 critical test, 0 passed, 1 failed
1 test total, 0 passed, 1 failed
==================================================================
Robot.Tests                                             | FAIL |
1 critical test, 0 passed, 1 failed
1 test total, 0 passed, 1 failed
```

```
Robot                                                         | FAIL |
1 critical test, 0 passed, 1 failed
1 test total, 0 passed, 1 failed
==================================================================
Output:    /Users/username/workspace/bank/output.xml
Log:       /Users/username/workspace/bank/log.html
Report:    /Users/username/workspace/bank/report.html
```

Here you can clearly see the failure is due to the expected value of 1000 not actually being displayed and was, in fact, 50. As you are using the WebTest library and Nosetest assertions underneath, Robot essentially passes up the underlying library's failure message for you to debug.

As you can see from the end of the output of the pybot test runner, it also outputs a few different files containing your test results. These files can be an easier way of debugging because they include log information and clearly highlight the areas that caused an issue. After running your tests, open report.html to see a clear breakdown of your test execution, such as the example shown in Figure 7-1. The other file of interest is the output.xml, which can be used by Jenkins plug-ins to display and track your test results in your build job. Chapter 10 covers more about this topic.

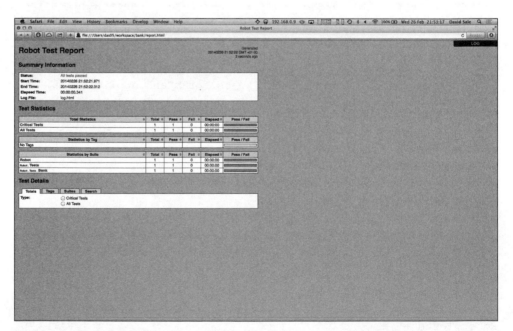

FIGURE 7-1: Example report.html generated during a Robot test execution.

Hopefully, from the examples shown here, you can see that the Robot framework offers a good alternative to Lettuce as an acceptance testing tool. Both offer you the capability to include libraries of established code within your tests and to write tailored Python code to support any test cases you may need to write. Both are explained in this book, with only a slight personal preference to Lettuce for its ease of use and similarity to the hugely popular Cucumber library. However, now that you've seen both tools, you can decide which is most suitable for your team and project.

Summary

This chapter looked to enable you to take your acceptance testing further. The chapter opened by providing you some of the background to acceptance testing's history and development of the Cucumber library. With this background, you can understand some of the influences and decisions that have led to the availability of tools like Lettuce and Robot in the Python community.

The chapter went on to bolster your everyday development skills using Lettuce by explaining the use and implementation of tagging. Tagging improves practices in Agile teams, by allowing QA testers and developers to create acceptance tests before writing any code and checking those tests in without fear of breaking the build. The tests can then have the tag removed when the test is passing after the code has been developed. Other practices, such as failing the test runner fast when it encounters a failure and Nosetest integration, were also introduced.

Finally, the chapter showed you an alternative to the tools discussed in earlier chapters and introduced the Robot test framework. An established, well-maintained library with plenty of support, Robot offers a great alternative to Lettuce should it suit your style of testing. The chapter showed how easy it is to write or even convert test cases and make use of other great tools such as WebTest under the hood. Should you wish to increase your learning on any of the topics covered, check out these additional helpful resources.

Resources

Gherkin Syntax Definition (for example, `Given`, `When`, `Then`): `https://github.com/ cucumber/cucumber/wiki/Gherkin`

Cucumber: `http://cukes.info`

Robot Framework: `http://robotframework.org`

Lettuce Nose Plug-in: `https://github.com/passy/nose-lettuce`

Chapter **8**
Maximizing Your Code's Performance

SO FAR, THIS book has stressed the importance of testing your application from every possible angle to ensure that your code works as expected and delivers quality to your end users or customers. Including a thorough testing process in your development cycle helps you deliver a product that meets your clients' needs. What hasn't been covered so far is how you can ensure that the code you write will actually perform under real-world conditions.

Say you are creating an HTTP service to deliver some data; the code you write for this service may perform well in the small-scale testing you do at the unit level. How will your application perform when you scale up from only a couple of requests per second to thousands, hundreds of thousands, and possibly millions? This is where performance testing comes into play and in particular the use of the JMeter tool. JMeter allows you to mimic some of the real-world conditions you expect your application to face to reveal the kind of response times your application will deliver by generating load on your application. As you scale up the amount of requests per second, is there a tipping point where suddenly the response times increase and performance suffers?

These are the kinds of questions you can answer with performance testing, which ideally takes place before your application has reached your end users. This gives you a chance to optimize your application's performance, using the code profiling tool CProfile to help find the areas in your code that are causing slower performance. With these optimizations in place you can then deliver the best possible customer experience for your product.

Understanding the Importance of Performance Testing

The performance of your application really can be a deciding factor in whether a customer enjoys using your application over a competitor's. This applies at all levels of your application, whether developing a backend service, middleware, or frontend service. The performance at every level contributes to your customers' perception. By developing a suite of repeatable performance tests, you can receive rapid feedback on the impact of changes you make. The various testing suites this book has introduced allow you to build confidence in the product to be released as it moves through a pipeline from unit testing to acceptance testing and finally performance testing before reaching your customer base. Leaving performance problems to be discovered only in a production environment is far from ideal. This can often result in callouts in the middle of the night for many members of the development team trying to figure out what the problem is. If you can find performance problems early, during normal working hours you'll have a much happier development team.

Performance testing also helps you plan various parts of your application and can influence design decisions. How does your application perform on a cloud environment versus a non-cloud environment? Do you need the capability to scale up and down quickly? How many instances of your application do you need to run to cope with an average amount of traffic? All these questions raise issues around costs and procurement. Your project's budget may allow only a certain amount of space in the cloud. You may have software or hardware limits and so your application must be as performative as possible to make best use of your available resources. Some problems cannot be overcome simply by throwing as much hardware at them as possible. Finding performance issues such as blocking I/O calls, lock contention, and CPU intensive operations allows you to refactor code and perhaps find a better alternative than the initial solution.

JMeter and Python

There are many ways to undertake performance testing your Python application, ranging from coding a small application that will cause many requests to your real application that is to be delivered to using established tools such as JMeter to generate the load on your application. This chapter focuses on the use of JMeter to build up testing plans you execute to generate the test load on your application and then use to analyze the results. By using JMeter, you also benefit from a range of documentation and support that is built up around this long-standing application. Although JMeter is written in Java, you don't need to know any Java code. You simply need to learn about the fields and options the tool provides to be able to build your test plan. You can then save your test plans, most likely in a source control repository, and reuse them to test your application as it is developed.

Released under an open-source license, JMeter is part of the Apache software foundation and was first released in December 1998. The application has undergone a vast amount of development in that time, leading to the robust tool widely used throughout development communities today. You can find the documentation for the tool on the JMeter website at `https://jmeter.apache.org`. The site includes a vast array of supporting information, such as best practices and FAQs. If you plan to set up performance testing following this book, I recommend you take time to go through the material available on the JMeter website. Alternatively, if you would like to come to grips with the application itself, jump ahead to the installation section.

Installation

Installing JMeter should be fairly straightforward on most machines. If you are using a Linux operating system such as Ubuntu, you can install JMeter using your package manager:

```
$ sudo apt-get install jmeter
```

Similarly, if using Apple's OS X, I recommend that you obtain Brew, which is a package manager for OS X. Information and installation instructions for Brew can be found at `http://brew.sh`. Once you have Brew, installing JMeter is as simple as this:

```
$ brew install jmeter
```

After you install JMeter, you can launch the application by running the `jmeter` command from the command line and you will launch into the JMeter interface, which you can see in Figure 8-1.

FIGURE 8-1: From JMeter's initial interface on first launch, you can define test plans.

Configuring Your Test Plans

Building the test plans for your application is easy and essentially involves adding elements to your JMeter test plan and providing a small amount of configuration. For the test plan you are going to build, you need to download and install an additional plug-in set that provides some useful test elements for you to use. To install the plug-in, you simply download the zip file and extract it into the correct folder.

The plug-in zip file can be downloaded from `http://jmeter-plugins.org/downloads/file/JMeterPlugins-1.0.0.zip`. If you discover that this version has been removed, visit `http://jmeter-plugins.org` and download the latest version of JMeterPlugins-Standard.

With the zip file downloaded, you simply extract it to the correct location. For Linux this will be wherever you downloaded the JMeter installation, and then you place the files into the `/lib/ext` folder. For Mac, if downloaded through Brew, then the correct path to extract to will be `/usr/local/Cellar/jmeter/2.11/libexec/lib/ext`.

With the plug-ins installed, first restart JMeter so it can detect the new plug-in. You can now begin to build up the test plan. To add your first element to the plan, right-click on Test Plan in the left pane, and choose Add⇨Config Element⇨HTTP Request Defaults. You can enter a base URL. For the bank application, enter `localhost` for the server name and the port is `5000`. This sets the base URL that JMeter will use for all requests. (See Figure 8-2.)

FIGURE 8-2: Add the HTTP Request Default element and set the base URL for requests.

Following this, you can add a thread group and set the number of threads that will make requests to your application. Essentially, this allows you to set the number of users interacting with your application. Add the thread group by right-clicking Test Plan again and choose Add⇨Threads (Users)⇨Thread Group. You can then enter the users; in this case, choose 20. Make sure to check the Loop Count Forever box, because this will allow you to control the time and number of requests via the plug-in you installed earlier. See Figure 8-3.

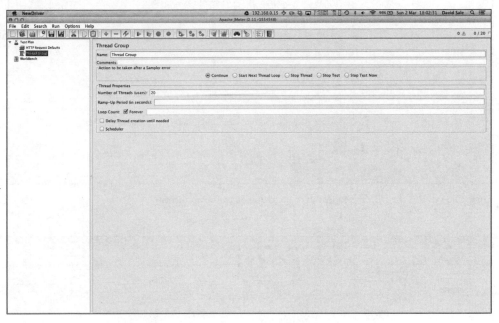

FIGURE 8-3: Add the Thread Group and set the number of application users to 20.

With the thread group in place, you can add the elements, which will handle making the requests to the application that you wish to performance test. In this example, you will be hitting the application root for the account 1111 that will then display a balance of 50. This request tests the performance of the account lookup and result rendering process. To do this, you add HTTP Request to your Test Plan by right-clicking Thread Group and choosing Add⇨Sampler⇨HTTP Request. With the HTTP Request pane open, you define the path that the request will be made to. Because you defined the Base URL in the first step, you don't need to enter that information here—only the path. To make the request you need, add /?account_number=1111 to the Path field and ensure the method selected is GET. (See Figure 8-4.)

Next, add the View Results Tree element by right-clicking on Thread Group and choosing Add⇨Listener⇨View Results Tree. (See Figure 8-5.) This allows you to view the HTTP Requests it is making and check the status code and responses are as expected.

FIGURE 8-4: Add the HTTP Request to make requests to the application.

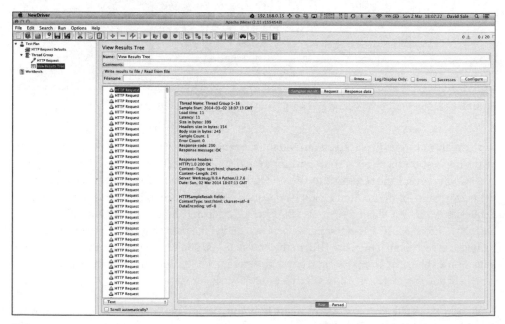

FIGURE 8-5: View the HTTP Requests to see that they are returning 200 OK status codes.

To execute a test plan, simply click the green play button toward the top of the JMeter application. You can then click around on the various views you have created to watch the results of the requests being made. One area of note when running a test is to ensure that the thread group you have created is enabled. You can do this by right-clicking on the thread group and choosing Enable. The thread group will show as greyed out in the sidebar if it is disabled.

The main work of the test plan is now in place to begin sending requests to your application. Now you need the four elements that allow you to view and analyze your data. To add them correctly, right-click on the Test Plan element at the top and find the name, as shown in the following list. Then apply any necessary configuration.

- **jjp@gc - Throughput Shaping Timer:** Found under Add⇨Timer, the shaping timer element allows you to configure the number of requests being made over a certain period of time and for how long. The configurations for this are almost endless and allow you to see the impact of a slow increase in requests to a very sudden, large increase in requests. Building the shape of requests in this way allows you to test your application's performance under different types of loads that it may encounter. To configure this, you add rows to the Request Per Second (RPS) Schedule table in the shaping timer view. You need to specify a start number of requests, an end number of requests, and a duration. So, for example, if you fill in 5,10,60, the requests ramp up evenly from 5 requests to 10 requests over a 60-second period. Figure 8-6 shows an example of the kind of shaping you can define for the requests in your application.

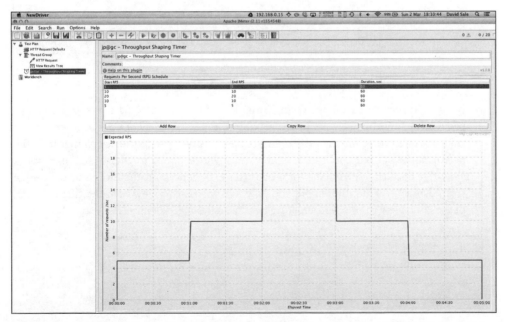

FIGURE 8-6: Example of the shaping timer stepping up the requests from 5 to 20 in 1-minute intervals.

- **jp@gc - Transactions per Second:** Found under Add⇨Listener, this element allows you to view the number of transactions being made per second. Transactions in this case are HTTP Requests. No configuration is needed for this element. It is merely an informational view of the data that JMeter is providing. You use this view combined with the Response Latencies Over Time element in the Composite graph to build up a picture of response time versus requests made. (See Figure 8-7.)

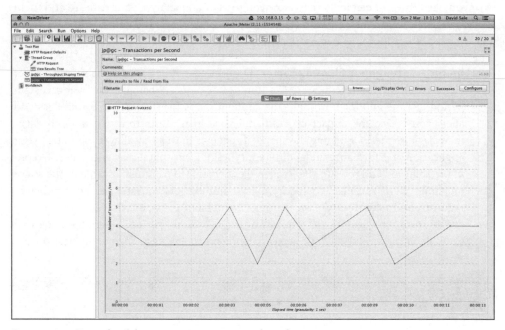

FIGURE 8-7: Example of the transactions-per-second graph view.

- **jp@gc - Response Latencies Over Time:** Found under Add⇨Listeners, this element provides you with another informational but important view of your JMeter data. It tracks the response times of the requests being made. One of the key elements in the performance of your application is how quickly it responds to your users' requests. A slow response time can make for a bad user experience and therefore put off people from using it. As mentioned previously, you combine this view with the transactions-per-second view for more interesting results analysis. (See Figure 8-8.)

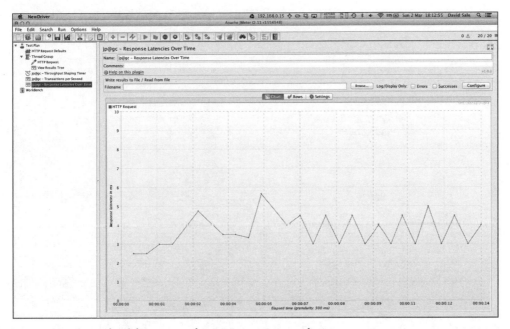

FIGURE 8-8: Example of the response latencies over time graph view.

- **jp@gc - Composite Graph:** Found under Add⇨Listener, the Composite Graph is the most important element of your test plan, where your key data is combined and can be analyzed for patterns or trends in the data. This graph shows you the response times of your application requests against the number of requests being made at that time. With this view of your data, you are able to see if there is any correlation between an increase/decrease in response times and the requests being made. Following such analysis, you can draw some conclusions about whether you need to refactor your code, perform more analysis to confirm the issue, introduce more hardware, or spin up more instances of your application to combat any problems your application is having. (See Figure 8-9.)

The composite graph requires some configuration. You essentially tell it which graphs to combine. You can see an example of the configuration in Figure 8-9, but to apply the configuration you need to navigate to the Composite Graph Graphs pane. Then click the right arrow on the HTTP Request (Success) transactions per second graph and the Overall Response Latencies from the response latencies over time graph. If you run your tests by hitting Play at the top and clicking on the Chart view for the composite graph, JMeter draws the two graphs together for you to analyze, as shown in Figure 8-10.

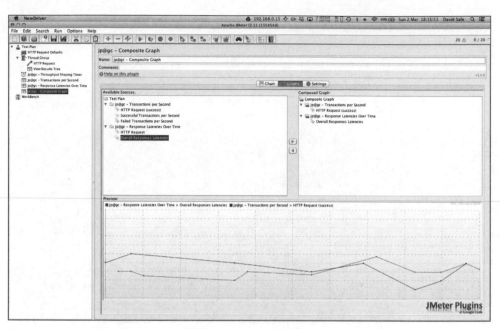

FIGURE 8-9: Example configuration for the composite graph view.

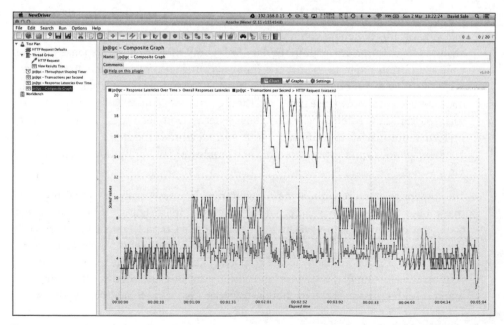

FIGURE 8-10: This combined graph view shows response times versus requests per second.

Utilizing Your Test Plans Effectively

You have brought together your first test plan and should be a little more comfortable with some of JMeter's key features. The next steps are to make good use of your performance testing to help drive better development and performance of your application. You can try making different requests to your application, ideally covering at least the main transaction through your app. Try testing the performance of each transaction in isolation to see the behavior of each individual journey. Following this, test the performance when each transaction is getting five requests per second. Does the application behavior change in any way under these differing scenarios? Testing thoroughly and across all possible eventualities gives you confidence in the end product you deliver.

Another technique you can use to gather even more statistics and data about your application is to combine your JMeter performance testing with other tools available on the market, including performance and analytics tools such as New Relic and App Dynamics. These tools are usually web-based and require an agent to be deployed with your application. The agent sends real-time data from your application to the servers of the tool where they present the data on the website front end. The main focus of these tools is usually monitoring an application in real time in a production environment. However there is no reason you can't set up a test or pre-production environment to deploy your application to, enable the monitoring tool, and analyze the traffic that is generated by your JMeter tests in the monitoring tool. The advantages of such an approach are that these tools normally have deep analytics that you can run to uncover the slow areas of your code and even provide method names and line numbers of suspect code. These are powerful weapons to have in your armory and could potentially save you from spending hours trolling through code to pinpoint exactly what the problem might be.

I wrote an article on this very subject for NetTuts; if you want to read more about this advanced technique, you can find it at `http://code.tutsplus.com/tutorials/new-relic-jmeter-perfect-performance-testing--net-34978`.

Code Profiling with cProfile

A lower level, perhaps rudimentary way of getting performance statistics from your code is through the use of code profiling tools. Python actually ships a code profiler as part of the standard library known as cProfile. With cProfile already available to you, you can dive straight into profiling your code and getting some stats. By using these tools, you can glean useful performance information, such as which methods and classes have the most calls. You can also get information such as the time spent in those methods, so by using these stats you can determine problem areas in your code that you could perhaps refactor and break down into more efficient calls.

cProfile is an invasive tool. It looks into every call that your application is making, including deep into the Python standard library and any other libraries you have installed. The output can be quite daunting to a new user, but it is a good way to learn what Python is doing underneath the code that you write. However, with a bit of knowledge about what your application is doing, and some of the code from the libraries you are importing, it's easy to make sense of the profiling report that cProfile can produce. You can also combine cProfile with some other tools to provide a different view of the output, which you can see later in the chapter.

Run a cProfile Session

cProfile is included as part of the Python standard library so there is no action you need to take other than installing Python on your machine to make use of this tool. cProfile provides a couple of ways to run a profile session on your code. The first option is to import the cProfile module and call its `run` method within your application's run code. Here's an example using the bank application from previous chapters:

```python
from flask import Flask, render_template, request

from account import Account
from bank import Bank

app = Flask(__name__)
BANK = Bank()

@app.route('/')
def hello_world():
    account_number = request.args.get('account_number')
    balance = BANK.get_account_balance(account_number)
    return render_template('index.html', balance=balance)

if __name__ == '__main__':
    account = Account('1111', 50)
    BANK.add_account(account)
    app.run(debug=True)
```

This code creates your Flask application, registers the root view, creates the bank instance, adds a test account, and finally, contains the main block at the end to start up the Flask development server so you can run your web application. If you want to profile your application from within this code, you can tweak the main block to wrap the starting of the application with cProfile.

```
if __name__ == '__main__':
    import cProfile

    account = Account('1111', 50)
    BANK.add_account(account)
    cProfile.run('app.run(debug=True)')
```

Notice how the Flask run statement is passed as a string to the cProfiler, because this method uses the Python exec command underneath to execute your code within the context of the profiler. If you run your application from the command line, make a request to the homepage, and then press **Ctrl+C** to kill your application. Upon closing the application cProfile outputs some stats on the code. (The last column usually contains the function name also, but this has been removed to allow for better formatting):

```
$ python bank_app.py
 * Running on http://127.0.0.1:5000/
 * Restarting with reloader
127.0.0.1 - - [02/Mar/2014 21:19:02] "GET /?account_number=1111
HTTP/1.1" 200 -
^C          14417 function calls (14238 primitive calls) in 3.286
Seconds
    Ordered by: standard name
    ncalls  tottime  percall  cumtime  percall filename:lineno
         1    0.000    0.000    3.286    3.286 <string>:1(<module>)
         1    0.000    0.000    0.000    0.000
BaseHTTPServer.py:102
         1    0.000    0.000    0.000    0.000
BaseHTTPServer.py:114
         1    0.000    0.000    0.000    0.000 BaseHTTPServer.py:18
         1    0.000    0.000    0.000    0.000 SocketServer.py:120
         1    0.000    0.000    0.000    0.000 SocketServer.py:160
         1    0.000    0.000    0.000    0.000 SocketServer.py:358
         1    0.000    0.000    0.000    0.000 SocketServer.py:480
         1    0.000    0.000    0.000    0.000 SocketServer.py:506
         1    0.000    0.000    0.000    0.000 SocketServer.py:579
         1    0.000    0.000    0.000    0.000 SocketServer.py:607
         1    0.000    0.000    0.000    0.000 SocketServer.py:608
         1    0.000    0.000    0.000    0.000 SocketServer.py:610
         1    0.000    0.000    0.000    0.000 SocketServer.py:611
         1    0.000    0.000    0.000    0.000 SocketServer.py:615
         1    0.000    0.000    0.000    0.000 SocketServer.py:618
         1    0.000    0.000    0.000    0.000 SocketServer.py:621
```

```
1      0.000      0.000      0.000      0.000  SocketServer.py:623
1      0.000      0.000      0.000      0.000  SocketServer.py:625
1      0.000      0.000      0.000      0.000  SocketServer.py:671
1      0.000      0.000      0.000      0.000  SocketServer.py:714
2      0.000      0.000      0.000      0.000  UserDict.py:18
2      0.000      0.000      0.000      0.000  UserDict.py:58
2      0.000      0.000      0.000      0.000  UserDict.py:70
```

This is just a snippet of the output that cProfile produces; it can get quite large because the profiler is looking at the underlying Python library code that you are importing and using in the application. The output the profiler has given you is not much use. Most of the modules it is producing stats on are not of interest to you because they aren't within your control and the application seems to have spent very little time in this code. Fortunately, the cProfile run method allows you to pass in a sort argument to specify how to order the results when presented to you. This means you can order the modules by those that the code spent most time in.

```
if __name__ == '__main__':
    import cProfile

    account = Account('1111', 50)
    BANK.add_account(account)
    cProfile.run('app.run(debug=True)', sort='time')
```

Now, when you execute the application, you get much more useful output showing statistics on methods you have actually developed:

```
$ python bank_app.py
 * Running on http://127.0.0.1:5000/
 * Restarting with reloader
127.0.0.1 - - [02/Mar/2014 21:32:21] "GET /?account_number=1111
                                      HTTP/1.1" 200 -
127.0.0.1 - - [02/Mar/2014 21:32:22] "GET /?account_number=1111
                                      HTTP/1.1" 200 -
127.0.0.1 - - [02/Mar/2014 21:32:23] "GET /?account_number=1111
                                      HTTP/1.1" 200 -
^C          23929 function calls (23750 primitive calls)
            in 8.700 seconds

    Ordered by: internal time
```

```
   ncalls    tottime   percall   cumtime   percall   filename:lineno
        9      8.629     0.959     8.629     0.959
     3852      0.032     0.000     0.032     0.000
     1935      0.007     0.000     0.041     0.000   serving.py:489
        1      0.006     0.006     8.693     8.693   serving.py:507
3433/3414      0.004     0.000     0.011     0.000
     1926      0.003     0.000     0.022     0.000   genericpath.py:26
     1926      0.002     0.000     0.002     0.000   stat.py:49
        1      0.001     0.001     0.004     0.004   serving.py:37
     2130      0.001     0.000     0.001     0.000
       19      0.001     0.000     0.008     0.000
    45/20      0.001     0.000     0.003     0.000   sre_parse.py:379
        1      0.001     0.001     0.002     0.002   subprocess.py:387
     1926      0.001     0.000     0.001     0.000   stat.py:24
       26      0.001     0.000     0.001     0.000   sre_compile.py:207
      696      0.001     0.000     0.001     0.000   sre_parse.py:182
        2      0.001     0.000     0.002     0.001   message.py:5
    66/16      0.000     0.000     0.002     0.000   sre_compile.py:32
        1      0.000     0.000     0.001     0.001   console.py:10
        1      0.000     0.000     0.003     0.003   __init__.py:10
        1      0.000     0.000     0.000     0.000   audio.py:5
        7      0.000     0.000     0.000     0.000   sre_compile.py:258
        1      0.000     0.000     0.004     0.004   feedparser.py:20
        1      0.000     0.000     0.001     0.001   pickle.py:25
        1      0.000     0.000     8.700     8.700   app.py:722
        1      0.000     0.000     0.002     0.002   tbtools.py:10
        1      0.000     0.000     0.001     0.001   charset.py:6
      615      0.000     0.000     0.001     0.000   sre_parse.py:201
        1      0.000     0.000     0.000     0.000   image.py:5
       2792 function calls (2714 primitive calls) in 8.823
seconds
```

Because the application you are profiling here is quite small, the most time-consuming calls are in the Flask library code, some of the profiler code itself, and some low level methods such as dictionary lookup methods like get. If you try running the profiler on some more substantial code where you are trying to find performance issues, you are likely to find more interesting results that you can act upon.

If you don't have a main method such as the preceding example to start your application, to run the profile you pass the cProfile library as a parameter to Python when calling your Python script:

```
$ python -m cProfile bank_app.py
 * Running on http://127.0.0.1:5000/
 * Restarting with reloader
```

```
127.0.0.1 - - [02/Mar/2014 21:39:19] "GET /?account_number=1111
                                     HTTP/1.1" 200 -
^C         55632 function calls (53686 primitive calls)
           in 10.961 seconds

   Ordered by: standard name

   ncalls  tottime  percall  cumtime  percall filename:lineno
        1    0.000    0.000    0.000    0.000 <string>:1
        1    0.000    0.000    0.000    0.000 <string>:1
        1    0.000    0.000    0.000    0.000 <string>:1
        1    0.000    0.000    0.000    0.000 <string>:1
        1    0.000    0.000    0.000    0.000 <string>:1
        1    0.000    0.000    0.000    0.000 <string>:1
        1    0.000    0.000    0.000    0.000 <string>:1(
        1    0.000    0.000    0.000    0.000 <string>:1
        1    0.000    0.000    0.000    0.000 <string>:1
        1    0.000    0.000    0.000    0.000 <string>:1
        1    0.000    0.000    0.000    0.000
BaseHTTPServer.py:102
        1    0.000    0.000    0.000    0.000
BaseHTTPServer.py:114
        1    0.000    0.000    0.000    0.000 BaseHTTPServer.py:18
        1    0.000    0.000    0.000    0.000 SocketServer.py:120
```

Again, you can control the order of the output by passing in the -s flag and an argument such as time by which to order (you can find more information on the options you can pass here at https://docs.python.org/2/library/profile.html#the-stats-class):

```
$ python -m cProfile -s time bank_app.py
 * Running on http://127.0.0.1:5000/
 * Restarting with reloader
127.0.0.1 - - [02/Mar/2014 21:40:25] "GET /?account_number=1111
                                     HTTP/1.1" 200 -
^C         55632 function calls (53686 primitive calls) in
           5.361 seconds

   Ordered by: internal time

   ncalls  tottime  percall  cumtime  percall filename:lineno
        2    5.244    2.622    5.244    2.622
   345/62    0.007    0.000    0.018    0.000 sre_parse.py:379
```

```
        226    0.005    0.000    0.008    0.000 sre_compile.py:207
          1    0.005    0.005    0.033    0.033 http.py:18
     613/57    0.004    0.000    0.014    0.000 sre_compile.py:32
          9    0.004    0.000    0.005    0.001 collections.py:288
       3738    0.004    0.000    0.004    0.000 sre_parse.py:182
          1    0.003    0.003    0.016    0.016 utils.py:5
          1    0.003    0.003    0.003    0.003
         51    0.002    0.000    0.002    0.000 sre_compile.py:258
          1    0.002    0.002    0.002    0.002 socket.py:45
          1    0.002    0.002    0.024    0.024 app.py:10
          1    0.002    0.002    0.002    0.002 _compat.py:1
          1    0.002    0.002    0.003    0.003 random.py:40
          1    0.002    0.002    0.002    0.002 __init__.py:4
    854/303    0.002    0.000    0.002    0.000 sre_parse.py:140
          1    0.002    0.002    0.003    0.003 datastructures.py:10
          1    0.002    0.002    0.013    0.013 environment.py:10
       2600    0.002    0.000    0.003    0.000 sre_parse.py:130
          1    0.001    0.001    0.005    0.005 urllib.py:23
       3020    0.001    0.000    0.005    0.000 sre_parse.py:201
          1    0.001    0.001    0.003    0.003 serving.py:37
          1    0.001    0.001    0.022    0.022 _internal.py:10
 12210/11866   0.001    0.000    0.001    0.000
         71    0.001    0.000    0.001    0.000
          1    0.001    0.001    0.061    0.061 exceptions.py:59
       7871    0.001    0.000    0.001    0.000
     223/60    0.001    0.000    0.018    0.000 sre_parse.py:301
          1    0.001    0.001    0.013    0.013 json.py:10
          1    0.001    0.001    0.004    0.004 itsdangerous.py:11
          1    0.001    0.001    0.002    0.002 subprocess.py:387
          1    0.001    0.001    0.103    0.103 __init__.py:11
          1    0.001    0.001    0.038    0.038 wrappers.py:22
          1    0.001    0.001    0.014    0.014 __init__.py:28
          1    0.001    0.001    0.019    0.019 inspect.py:25
          2    0.001    0.000    0.001    0.000 _compat.py:12
          1    0.001    0.001    0.005    0.005 routing.py:97
       2829    0.001    0.000    0.001    0.000
```

The results between the two ways of running the profiling session are virtually identical and it is really a matter of which method of executing the cProfiler works best for your code and application setup.

Analyzing the cProfile Output

The documentation for the cProfile library is extensive and provides many examples and explanations for scenarios that may arise in your profiling session. Check the resources for links to relevant information at the end of the chapter, but meanwhile, here is a summary of the key points.

If you take a snippet of the cProfile output from the Bank application example, you can break down some of the information it is trying to convey to you:

```
55632 function calls (53686 primitive calls) in
5.361 seconds

    Ordered by: internal time

    ncalls  tottime  percall  cumtime  percall
    filename:lineno(func)
         2    5.244    2.622    5.244    2.622 {posix.waitpid}
    345/62    0.007    0.000    0.018    0.000 sre_parse.py:379
       226    0.005    0.000    0.008    0.000 sre_compile.py:207
         1    0.005    0.005    0.033    0.033 http.py:18(<module>)
    613/57    0.004    0.000    0.014    0.000 sre_compile.py:32
         9    0.004    0.000    0.005    0.001 collections.py:288
      3738    0.004    0.000    0.004    0.000 sre_parse.py:182
         1    0.003    0.003    0.016    0.016 utils.py:5(<module>)
         1    0.003    0.003    0.003    0.003 {posix.read}
        51    0.002    0.000    0.002    0.000
```

The first line is an indicator of the number of functions that were actually executed during your profiling session. Primitive calls indicate those that are not recursive. The line also states the total time for the session. The headings for the table are broken down in the documentation, as follows:

- **ncalls:** The number of calls to the given function.

- **tottime:** The total time spent in the given function (and excluding time made in calls to sub-functions).

- **percall:** The quotient of tottime divided by ncalls.

- **cumtime:** The cumulative time spent in this and all sub-functions (from invocation till exit). This figure is accurate even for recursive functions.

- **percall:** The quotient of cumtime divided by primitive calls.

- **filename:lineno(function):** The respective data of each function.

If you'd like a more visual representation of the data, there is a great Python library called PyCallGraph. The library converts your cProfile session into a PNG image, showing the method calls grouped by library and even highlights those, which could be problem areas for your application. At the time of writing, the library is at version 1.0.1 and can be installed using the standard Pip installation process.

```
$ pip install pycallgraph
Downloading/unpacking pycallgraph
Successfully installed pycallgraph
Cleaning up...
```

Once installed, you can simply issue the following command to execute your application, run the cProfile session, and have PyCallGraph output the image file on exit of the application:

```
$ pycallgraph graphviz -- bank_app.py
 * Running on http://127.0.0.1:5000/
 * Restarting with reloader
127.0.0.1 - - [02/Mar/2014 22:07:24] "GET /?account_number=1111
  HTTP/1.1" 200 -
```

Upon exiting, the library created a file in the current directory called `pycallgraph.png`, which you can then open using any image application of your choice. The image can get quite large if your application is using many libraries and/or is quite complex. But you can zoom in on the details to get a better idea what it is calling. An example output for the Bank application is shown in Figure 8-11.

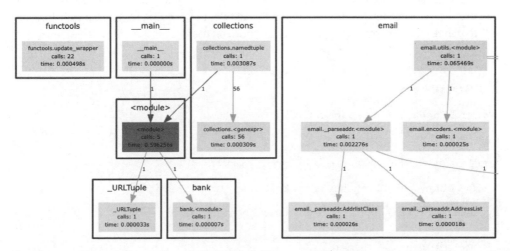

FIGURE 8-11: Example output from the pycallgraph library on the bank.py application.

Summary

This chapter focused on a key part of the testing life cycle in analyzing and reflecting upon the actual performance of your application under real-world scenarios. Unit testing and acceptance testing provide a firm foundation for the code and business logic, respectively. However, unless you undertake performance testing before going into production, you have no way of knowing how your application will behave under realistic load. Performance testing lets you find out about any issues you may have in your application *before* your users do. By combining powerful, established tools like JMeter and New Relic, you can establish a reusable testing suite, which all new release candidates must pass through before giving the go-ahead for a production release. This keeps real-time support to a minimum and helps add to the goal of having zero defects in production alongside the other forms of testing this book has covered.

cProfile is an alternative tool that lets you take an in-depth look at exactly how and where Python is spending its time when executing your code. The tool can be used in combination with other methods, such as JMeter, to confirm your suspicions around a slow method or line in a file. The fact that cProfile is baked into the Python distribution makes it easy for anyone to pick up and use it, and some great documentation makes it easy to learn and discuss with other Python developers. Some of the neat packages written around cProfile can provide you with great ways of analyzing the data, such as converting the stats tables into call graphs. PyCallGraph provides an excellent visual representation of your code's call hierarchy and clearly marks any problem code areas for your attention and further analysis.

This chapter has introduced you to or supported your knowledge of performance testing and the kind of benefits it can bring. It really is such an important process to undertake and is often overlooked at the end of projects, especially when deadlines need to be met. Ensure you build some time into your development schedule for performance testing to help yourself to deliver the best quality application for your end users.

Resources

JMeter: `https://jmeter.apache.org`

New Relic: `http://newrelic.com`

AppDynamics: `http://www.appdynamics.com`

cProfile: `http://docs.python.org/2/library/profile.html`

PyCallGraph: `http://pycallgraph.slowchop.com/en/master/`

Chapter 9

Looking After Your Lint

THIS CHAPTER IS covers the routine housekeeping tasks for your application and the tools you need to help keep your code in check. The creator of Python himself, Guido, along with some other key developers of the language, encourage Python developers to follow certain style guidelines. These guidelines and other suggestions and information about the language are conveyed to the global Python community via Python Enhancement Proposal (PEP) documents. Guido created the famous PEP-8 document in which most of the Python style guidelines are defined. Elements such as indentation, naming conventions, instance properties, and many other code factors have specific instructions in PEP-8. Following these suggestions makes your code more readable and accessible to Python developers around the world.

Fortunately, tools have been developed to increase confidence in your code meeting these guidelines. Pylint—a Python package that can be installed using Pip on the command line—offers a convenient way to check your code and suggests where your code has not met expectations. Fix the errors Pylint finds to ensure your application's code meets the expectations of the language and the Python development community.

Finally, this chapter tells you how to ensure your application's code has full code coverage. Unit tests are a vital part of your testing, but if areas of your application aren't covered by tests then you are leaving yourself vulnerable to a defect in production. Covering all parts of the application that you can establishes some confidence that you have tested your application appropriately. Furthermore, by adding code coverage statistics as part of your build process, you create a tracking metric as development continues to ensure your level of coverage remains high.

Coming to Grips with Pylint

Getting started with Pylint is relatively simple but does require a little configuration to tailor it to your exact needs. Pylint is a Python package that can be installed using pip on the command line. At the time of writing, the latest version of Pylint is 1.2.1, released on April 30, 2014—an indication that the package is maintained quite regularly.

Installing Pylint

To install Pylint, add the following line to your requirements file and pip install:

```
pylint==1.2.1
$ pip install -r requirements.txt
```

Alternatively, you can install the package directly:

```
$ pip install pylint==1.2.1
```

Using Pylint

With Pylint installed, you can execute the tool from the command line, providing your Python application as an argument. By default, Pylint will create a report showing some of the areas in your code that do not meet the PEP-8 defined standard. It then breaks the report down with more information, such as message type, the number of occurrences of each type of message, and a breakdown of the dependencies of your application. To run the Pylint tool with just its default configuration, execute the following on the command line. Again, you can use the bank application as a test area.

> The following command analyzes only the `bank_app.py` file. To run Pylint across your whole project, pass the top-level directory as the argument to Pylint and it will recursively search down the directory tree for Python files to check.

Execute Pylint on the command line.

```
$ pylint bank/bank_app.py
```

You will then see the following output:

```
No config file found, using default configuration
************* Module bank.bank_app
C: 16, 0: Final newline missing (missing-final-newline)
C:  1, 0: Missing module docstring (missing-docstring)
```

```
W:  2, 0: Relative import 'bank',
            should be 'bank.bank' (relative-import)
W:  3, 0: Relative import 'account',
            should be 'bank.account' (relative-import)
C:  4, 0: Invalid constant name "app" (invalid-name)
C:  8, 0: Missing function docstring (missing-docstring)
C: 14, 4: Invalid constant name "account" (invalid-name)

Report
======
14 statements analyzed.

Messages by category
--------------------
```

```
+-----------+-------+---------+-----------+
|type       |number |previous |difference |
+===========+=======+=========+===========+
|convention |5      |5        |=          |
+-----------+-------+---------+-----------+
|refactor   |0      |0        |=          |
+-----------+-------+---------+-----------+
|warning    |2      |2        |=          |
+-----------+-------+---------+-----------+
|error      |0      |0        |=          |
+-----------+-------+---------+-----------+
```

```
Messages
--------
```

```
+----------------------+------------+
|message id            |occurrences |
+======================+============+
|relative-import       |2           |
+----------------------+------------+
|missing-docstring     |2           |
+----------------------+------------+
|invalid-name          |2           |
+----------------------+------------+
|missing-final-newline |1           |
+----------------------+------------+
```

```
Global evaluation
-----------------
Your code has been rated at 5.00/10 (previous run: 5.00/10, +0.00)

Duplication
-----------

+------------------------+------+---------+-----------+
|                        |now   |previous |difference |
+========================+======+=========+===========+
|nb duplicated lines     |0     |0        |=          |
+------------------------+------+---------+-----------+
|percent duplicated lines|0.000 |0.000    |=          |
+------------------------+------+---------+-----------+


Raw metrics
-----------

+----------+-------+-------+---------+-----------+
|type      |number |%      |previous |difference |
+==========+=======+=======+=========+===========+
|code      |15     |100.00 |15       |=          |
+----------+-------+-------+---------+-----------+
|docstring |0      |0.00   |0        |=          |
+----------+-------+-------+---------+-----------+
|comment   |0      |0.00   |0        |=          |
+----------+-------+-------+---------+-----------+
|empty     |0      |0.00   |0        |=          |
+----------+-------+-------+---------+-----------+


Statistics by type
------------------

+----------+-------+-----------+-----------+------------+---------+
|type      |number |old number |difference |%documented |%badname |
+==========+=======+===========+===========+============+=========+
|module    |1      |1          |=          |0.00        |0.00     |
+----------+-------+-----------+-----------+------------+---------+
|class     |0      |0          |=          |0           |0        |
+----------+-------+-----------+-----------+------------+---------+
|method    |0      |0          |=          |0           |0        |
+----------+-------+-----------+-----------+------------+---------+
|function  |1      |1          |=          |0.00        |0.00     |
+----------+-------+-----------+-----------+------------+---------+
```

```
External dependencies
---------------------
::

    bank
      \-account
      | \-Account (bank.bank_app)
      \-bank
        \-Bank (bank.bank_app)
    flask
      \-Flask (bank.bank_app)
      \-render_template (bank.bank_app)
      \-request (bank.bank_app)
```

As you can see, Pylint offers great insight into your code and provides everything you need to fix your code to match the PEP-8 specification.

Understanding the Pylint Report

Breaking down the report that Pylint produces gives you a better sense of the information being presented.

The Module Block

The first section of the report and the information of most use to you is the module breakdown showing the actual Pylint errors. This block shows the areas of the code that are failing to meet some criteria of PEP-8 by line number, reason, and file/module name. In the preceding example, you can pick out one Pylint error to fix. The report shows the following:

```
************* Module bank.bank_app
C: 16, 0: Final newline missing (missing-final-newline)
```

This particular Pylint error is telling you that in the file bank/bank_app.py, at line 16, there is no new line at the end of the file, which is one of the PEP-8 style recommendations. If you add a new line to that file and run the Pylint tool again, the tool doesn't report this anymore. Make this Pylint feature your go-to tool for finding and fixing errors.

The Messages by Category Section

In this section of the report, Pylint organizes the errors it is instructing you to fix by their category. For example, one Pylint error you may come across is too many parameters for a method. An error such as this would fall under the refactor category, suggesting you break down the method into smaller methods with fewer responsibilities. The previous new line at the end of a file error would fall under the convention category. This area of the report also gives you an overview of which parts of the PEP-8 standards you are not following, so you can follow up and get the details from the first section of the report.

The Messages Section

The messages section of the report details each message type and the number of occurrences of that Pylint error in your code. It can be useful to check this, because you may discover multiple instances of a specific error. If you find you are always creating a certain Pylint error, read more information about it to avoid making it when you write your code, so Pylint will not need to keep reminding you to fix it.

The Code Evaluation Score

Pylint gives your code a score. The closer your score is to 10, the freer it is of Pylint errors, which you should aim for. Pylint uses the following formula to calculate this score, you should notice that any category of error will harm your score:

```
10.0 - ((float(5 * error + warning + refactor + convention) /
  statement) * 10)
```

The Raw Metrics Section

This section shows you the various areas of the code and the number and proportion of Pylint errors. For example, the errors may be in the main Python code, or in other areas such as docstrings or comments.

The Statistics by Type Section

Another breakdown view of the report, in this section of Pylint, shows what the analyzed code is made up of. For example, `bank_app.py` is one module and has one function. If the tool runs across your entire application (more on this later in this chapter), you will get a detailed look at how your application is structured.

Customizing Pylint's Output

While the default behavior of Pylint is useful enough, it actually provides a great number of customization options. All the Pylint customization can be handled in the config file `pylintrc`, which is placed in the root directory of your project for Pylint to pick up and use. There are many things you can set for the output such as customizing messages making the line numbers and modules names more readable, or suppressing certain errors, and so forth. The first step in customizing your output is to create a `pylintrc` file in the root folder of your project.

To customize the information when an error is found, for example to make it more readable, add the following:

```
[REPORTS]
msg-template="{msg_id}({symbol}) - {obj} Line #{line}: {msg}"
```

Now execute Pylint on the command line.

```
$ pylint bank/bank_app.py
```

This produces a much more readable format for checking what the Pylint errors are and where they came from:

```
************* Module bank.bank_app
C0304(missing-final-newline) -  Line #16: Final newline missing
C0111(missing-docstring) -  Line #1: Missing module docstring
W0403(relative-import) -  Line #2: Relative import 'bank',
                          should be 'bank.bank'
W0403(relative-import) -  Line #3: Relative import 'account',
                            should be 'bank.account'
C0103(invalid-name) -  Line #4: Invalid constant name "app"
C0111(missing-docstring) - hello_world Line #8: Missing
                                        function docstring
C0103(invalid-name) -  Line #14: Invalid constant name "account"
```

Another option you can add to the pylintrc file includes the capability to always ignore certain errors. For example, you may not want to follow the convention of having a new line at the end of every file, so to permanently disable that message you can add the following code to your pylintrc (you can add multiple by providing a comma-separated list):

```
[MESSAGES CONTROL]
# Use this to remove uninteresting (or currently
  less important) warnings and errors.
disable=C0304
```

Now execute Pylint on the command line.

```
$ pylint bank/bank_app.py
```

The new line at the end of a file warning has now been omitted.

```
************* Module bank.bank_app
C0111(missing-docstring) -  Line #1: Missing module docstring
W0403(relative-import) -  Line #2: Relative import 'bank',
                                    should be 'bank.bank'
W0403(relative-import) -  Line #3: Relative import 'account',
                                    should be 'bank.account'
C0103(invalid-name) -  Line #4: Invalid constant name "app"
C0111(missing-docstring) - hello_world Line #8: Missing
                                       function docstring
C0103(invalid-name) -  Line #14: Invalid constant name "account"
```

Another useful option is the capability to display only messages and none of the statistics or reports after that section. If you have no use for them or simply want to focus only on the error messages themselves, add the following option to the REPORTS heading:

```
reports=no
```

Finally, the last section of note in `pylintrc` is the Design section. Here you can override the default standards that the code is following. You can set your own limits on things like parameters to methods, indentations, return statements, and so on. Although there are good reasons to change some of these values, you may want to use this feature sparingly because you may diverge too far from the Python PEP-8 standards. It is provided here for your reference, however. The options presented here are an example; you can customize many options. A search on the Pylint documentation will help you find anything you may need to provide here. See the resources section for a link.

```
[DESIGN]
# Maximum number of arguments for function / method
max-args=5

# Argument names that match this expression
# will be ignored. Default to name with leading underscore
ignored-argument-names=_.*

# Maximum number of locals for function / method body
max-locals=15

# Maximum number of returns / yields for function / method body
max-returns=8

# Maximum number of branches for function / method body
max-branches=12
```

```
# Maximum number of statements in function / method body
max-statements=50

# Maximum number of parents for a class (see R0901).
max-parents=7

# Maximum number of attributes for a class (see R0902).
max-attributes=10
```

Telling Pylint to Ignore Errors

Pylint can find a great number of errors because the PEP-8 standard is quite large and covers many areas of the code style. There will inevitably be cases where you want the code to be a certain way for some valid reason, but Pylint will produce an error for it. Fortunately, you can ignore errors by placing a #pylint: disable=AXXX comment block into your code next to the offending line. Simply replace AXXX with the code that Pylint outputs in your newly customized Pylint error output and run Pylint again. Pylint ignores that particular error and moves on to the next one in your code.

The first step to telling Pylint to ignore an error is to locate that error in your Pylint report. From there, you can obtain the code that is required to be passed to the Pylint disable comment. If you run Pylint on the bank application, you can see some Pylint errors you can ignore.

```
$ pylint bank/bank_app.py
```

This produces the following output.

```
************* Module bank.bank_app
C0111(missing-docstring) -  Line #1: Missing module docstring
W0403(relative-import) -  Line #2: Relative import 'bank',
                              should be 'bank.bank'
W0403(relative-import) -  Line #3: Relative import 'account',
                                  should be 'bank.account'
C0103(invalid-name) -  Line #4: Invalid constant name "app"
C0111(missing-docstring) - hello_world Line #8: Missing
                                        function docstring
C0103(invalid-name) -  Line #14: Invalid constant name "account"
```

The last error is a good example of the type of error you want Pylint to ignore because you really do want to use the name "account" for this variable. Notice the line in your code, which is causing the Pylint error has the Pylint code of C0103 . To tell Pylint to ignore this error go to line 14 in `bank.bank_app.py` and add `#pylint: disable=C0103` as shown in the example below. Note that this only disables this single Pylint error message for this line in your code only.

```
13: if __name__ == '__main__':
14:     account = Account('1111', 50) #pylint: disable=C0103
15:     BANK.add_account(account)
16:     app.run(debug=True)
```

Now if you run the Pylint report again, the account variable is no longer reported as an error, as shown here:

```
$ pylint bank/bank_app.py
```

The command produces the following output.

```
************* Module bank.bank_app
I0011(locally-disabled) - Line #14: Locally disabling C0103
C0111(missing-docstring) -  Line #1: Missing module docstring
W0403(relative-import) -  Line #2: Relative import 'bank',
                                    should be 'bank.bank'
W0403(relative-import) -  Line #3: Relative import 'account',
                                    should be 'bank.account'
C0103(invalid-name) -  Line #4: Invalid constant name "app"
C0111(missing-docstring) - hello_world Line #8: Missing function
   docstring
```

Covering All Your Code with Unit Tests

As stressed earlier in the book and the beginning of this chapter, keeping your code completely covered by unit tests is vital to ensuring that defects and mistakes don't slip through the safety net that unit tests provide. Using tools such as Coverage ensures that you have metrics to prove that you have indeed covered every line of the code that can be tested via a unit test. Code coverage information is usually presented as a percentage for the full program, and also broken down into lines, methods, and classes that are covered. Having code coverage information in your testing and build process lets you monitor the coverage level to prevent areas of the code from going untested. The topic of code coverage was touched upon in Chapter 3. However, here you find a more detailed introduction to installing the Coverage tool, a recap of its integration with nosetest, and also advanced features and customization.

Installing Coverage

Installing Coverage follows the now familiar pip install format. The current version of Coverage is 3.7.1 and was released on December 13, 2013. There is a good amount of documentation around the tool, and extra help and support can be found on the official website for Coverage (`http://nedbatchelder.com/code/coverage/`). To install this version, use the following command:

```
$ pip install coverage==3.7.1
```

Alternatively, install the latest version by removing the version information:

```
$ pip install coverage
```

Using Coverage

The simplest method of using the Coverage tool is through integration in the nosetest tool. Running nosetest with the coverage option gives you a breakdown of the coverage report printed directly after the output of your tests. You can then add the nosetest coverage option into your build process when running your unit tests, to gather coverage information every time you run the build. Alternatively, you can execute from the command line, specifying the --with-coverage argument, like so:

```
$ nosetests --with-coverage
```

The command will produce the following output.

```
...
Name            Stmts    Miss   Cover   Missing
-------------------------------------------------
bank                1       0    100%
bank.account        4       0    100%
bank.bank           7       0    100%
bank.tools          1       0    100%
-------------------------------------------------
TOTAL              13       0    100%
-------------------------------------------------
Ran 3 tests in 0.018s

OK
```

The current state of the bank application looks good. Coverage is indicating that every line of the code is covered by a unit test. If you remove one unit test, you see how Coverage reports missing lines to you. Try commenting out one of the bank class tests:

```
# def test_get_account_balance(self):
#     bank = Bank()
#     self.assertEqual({}, bank.accounts)
#     self.assertEqual(len(bank.accounts), 0)
#
#     account_1 = Account(001, 50)
#
#     bank.add_account(account_1)
#
#     self.assertEqual(bank.get_account_balance(001), 50)
```

If you now run the Coverage tool with your unit tests, you are told which lines of the class are not covered by a test.

Be sure to remove the coverage file generated from any previous runs; otherwise, you will see inaccurate mixed results for your coverage report.

To remove the preceding coverage report, add the `--cover-erase` option. Run the following on the command line.

```
$ nosetests --with-coverage --cover-erase
```

The command will produce the following output.

```
..
Name            Stmts   Miss  Cover   Missing
-------------------------------------------
bank                1      0   100%
bank.account        4      0   100%
bank.bank           7      1    86%   9
bank.tools          1      0   100%
-------------------------------------------
TOTAL              13      1    92%
-------------------------------------------
Ran 2 tests in 0.019s
OK
```

After that removal, coverage report indicates that line 9 of the bank class is not covered by a test. If you inspect line 9 in the bank class, you can see it is actually the functionality that the test was checking, the `get_account_balance` method. Adding the test back in returns your code coverage to 100%.

Advanced Coverage Options

As with Pylint and other command-line Python tools, the Coverage tool has a few options to expand its usefulness. Some of the options that you can look at are producing HTML/XML reports of your coverage, setting a minimum threshold for your coverage percentage, and restricting coverage to certain packages you may be interested in.

Producing an HTML/XML Report

Outputting the coverage report in a different format that prints to the screen is simple. You have two options available to you: HTML and XML. The XML option is of use to third-party tools such as Jenkins, which can produce graphics and other views from the XML information. Creating the XML output from your coverage report is just a matter of adding another option to the command-line. This creates a file called `coverage.xml` in the directory from which you executed the nosetest command.

```
$ nosetests --with-coverage --cover-erase --cover-xml
```

The command produces the following output.

```
..

Name            Stmts   Miss  Cover   Missing
---------------------------------------------
bank                1      0   100%
bank.account        4      0   100%
bank.bank           7      1    86%   9
bank.tools          1      0   100%
---------------------------------------------
TOTAL              13      1    92%
---------------------------------------------
Ran 2 tests in 0.020s
OK
```

The HTML option produces a miniature website version of your report that allows you to click into your files and see whether lines are covered—indicated by green and red. Again, this is a nicer, more visual way of consuming the coverage report information and could be another build artifact of a continuous integration build of your project. The inclusion of such information allows developers and QAs to easy see status by visiting the continuous integration server and clicking through to explore the HTML version of the coverage report. Generating the HTML report again requires adding an option to the nosetests command. The report will be generated in a folder named `cover`, which will contain the HTML and CSS required to style the report. After creating the HTML report, open `index.html` in a browser to view a report similar to the one shown in Figure 9-1.

```
$ nosetests --with-coverage --cover-erase --cover-html
```

The command produces the following output.

```
..
Name             Stmts   Miss   Cover   Missing
------------------------------------------------
bank                 1      0   100%
bank.account         4      0   100%
bank.bank            7      1    86%   9
bank.tools           1      0   100%
------------------------------------------------
TOTAL               13      1    92%
------------------------------------------------
Ran 2 tests in 0.019s
OK
```

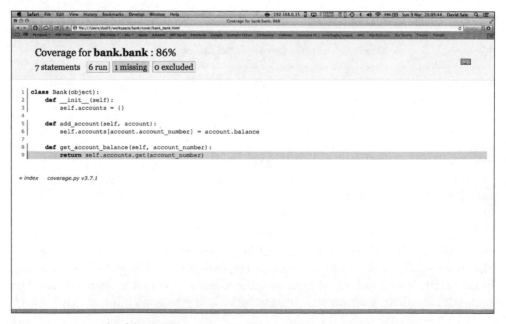

FIGURE 9-1: Example of the HTML from the Coverage tool showing an uncovered line.

Setting a Minimum Coverage Threshold

Setting a minimum threshold is a great option when you are working on a group or even personal project. It ensures that if the code coverage falls below the agreed level, your test/ build will fail, forcing the person who made the coverage level to fall to increase his or her test coverage. Once again, there is a command line option for nosetest execution to set the required threshold. The report will then mark at the end if the code coverage did not meet the minimum required level, as shown here:

```
$ nosetests --with-coverage --cover-erase --cover-min-percentage=95
```

The command produces the following output.

```
..
Name              Stmts   Miss  Cover   Missing
-----------------------------------------------
bank                  1      0   100%
bank.account          4      0   100%
bank.bank             7      1    86%   9
bank.tools            1      0   100%
-----------------------------------------------
TOTAL                13      1    92%
nose.plugins.cover: ERROR: TOTAL Coverage did
                    not reach minimum required: 95%
```

Restricting Coverage to a Specific Package

While developing the code, you may want to target your report to show the coverage for the particular section of the application you are working on at that moment in time. The Coverage tool provides an easy way to set a target for which the code coverage is analyzed. Adding the option to cover a package with the package name narrows down the report as required. For example, you could target the account package, like so:

```
$ nosetests --with-coverage --cover-erase

        --cover-package=bank.account
```

The command produces the following output.

```
..
Name              Stmts   Miss  Cover   Missing
-----------------------------------------------
bank.account          4      0   100%
-----------------------------------------------
Ran 2 tests in 0.020s
OK
```

Ignoring Coverage

Much like Pylint allows you to ignore error cases, coverage provides a way to add comments to your code if you want to omit a given line from the coverage report. You may want to do this on lines that you cannot realistically cover with a unit test. You should do this only if you are confident the code is tested in other ways, such as through acceptance tests, which the Coverage tool does not take into account. If you take the example used earlier, where the test for `get_account_balance` was commented out, which resulted in line 9 of the bank class becoming uncovered; you can see that adding the comment means the line is not shown as being uncovered any longer:

```
$ nosetests --with-coverage --cover-erase
```

The command produces the following output.

```
..
Name            Stmts   Miss  Cover   Missing
---------------------------------------------
bank                1      0   100%
bank.account        4      0   100%
bank.bank           7      1    86%   9
bank.tools          1      0   100%
---------------------------------------------
TOTAL              13      1    92%
---------------------------------------------
Ran 2 tests in 0.018s
OK
```

The line presently is uncovered, but you can now add a comment that will indicate to coverage to ignore this line from its report:

```
    def get_account_balance(self, account_number): #pragma: no
                                                    cover
        return self.accounts.get(account_number)
```

Running the report again shows you that you now have 100% coverage:

```
$ nosetests --with-coverage --cover-erase
```

The command produces the following output.

```
..
Name            Stmts   Miss   Cover   Missing
---------------------------------------------
bank                1      0    100%
bank.account        4      0    100%
bank.bank           5      0    100%
bank.tools          1      0    100%
---------------------------------------------
TOTAL              11      0    100%
---------------------------------------------
Ran 2 tests in 0.020s
OK
```

Summary

This chapter showed you the importance of good housekeeping around your code. Not only can Pylint ensure that your code follows the standards that Python developers and indeed the Python creator expect, but it also can make your code more readable, structured, and standardized. You were introduced to some useful Pylint customizations that allow you to tailor the tool to your needs. Formatting options, enforcing code style principles/decisions within your codebase, and case by case ignoring of errors allow you to use the tool according to your application and project requirements. As recommended, you should follow the defaults provided by Pylint as much as possible and only customize where necessary.

Coverage was also reintroduced. Producing coverage reports as part of your development cycle helps to ensures that there are no gaps in your testing, which minimizes the risk of defects reaching a production environment. Advanced options, such as setting a coverage threshold, keep the test coverage at the forefront of developers' minds when writing code and testing the build. Other options, such as producing HTML reports of the coverage state, enables access to this information for less technical personnel, such as scrum masters or technical analysts, who may be interested in such stats.

Following these good practices helps you produce a quality code base in terms of its accessibility and readability for other Python developers. The key is to automate these processes wherever possible and make them part of your build. Chapter 10 covers this practice of automation in detail.

Resources

Pylint: http://www.pylint.org

Pylint (PyPi page): http://www.pylint.org

Coverage: http://nedbatchelder.com/code/coverage/

Coverage (PyPi page): https://pypi.python.org/pypi/coverage

PEP-8 Document: http://www.python.org/dev/peps/pep-0008/

Chapter 10
Automating Your Processes

WITH A FIRM testing suite built up over the course of this book, it's now time to turn your attention to automating the tasks that surround your testing process. By automating as much as possible, you ensure that nothing in the testing suite is missed and you know that every time you make changes to the code base, those changes are going through the same stringent checks that the previous code had gone through. Having this in place early in your project means that as the application changes it continually goes through a pipeline of checks. As the code makes its way through this pipeline, you grow more confident that the application that you have created is ready for production and use by your customers.

Without automation, you will inevitably miss something. This chapter introduces you to some of the automation tools available to solve this problem. By creating tasks using the Python Paver tool and executing them upon every check-in with Jenkins, you can be certain that every test you write is executed each time. You also gain instant feedback if your tests fail for any reason. Jenkins also allows you to automate some more advanced ideas, such as deploying your code into environments on every passing build, known as continuous deployment, or combining with some of the tools introduced in previous chapters, such as coverage or PyLint to produce statistics and graphs for each build.

By the end of this chapter, you should feel comfortable creating Paver tasks to execute your tests and be able to define a default set of tasks to be executed as part of the build. You should be able to configure a basic build job in Jenkins, which will be executed each time you check into your code base and explore the output that Jenkins produces for each build. Finally, you will look at integrating those tools to get the maximum amount of information from your builds regarding how your code and tests look.

Build Paver Tasks

Previous chapters examined various testing tools, such as nosetest, Lettuce, Coverage, and PyLint, all of which are executed on the command line in various ways. This means that if you want to run the whole suite of testing that you have set up, you need to chain all your commands together using shell syntax or create custom aliases in your `.bashrc` to provide one command that runs them all. Fortunately, Paver provides a more standard and structured way of running all the different tools that you need for your project. It also provides a way of setting a default set of tasks that enables you to run your entire suite of tasks simply by executing `paver` from the command line. Best of all, the Paver task configuration can be checked in with your source code, meaning you do not need to manually configure each machine with your own custom commands. Instead, a developer can check out your code, install the project requirements, and run Paver to execute the test suite and check whether the development environment is setup correctly.

Installing Paver

Installing Paver follows much the same process for installing other Python packages. The latest version at the time of writing is 1.2.2, released on January 12, 2014. You can install the package in one of two ways. One way is to add the following line to your `requirements.txt` file, like so:

```
Paver==1.2.2
```

Or you can Pip install using either of the commands (the first will download the latest version at the time of installing), like so:

```
$ pip install paver
$ pip install paver==1.2.2
```

Creating a Paver Task

Writing a task is fairly simple. It requires adding a file named `pavement.py` to the root of your project directory. In this file, you define the Paver tasks that Paver will be able to execute. A good first Paver task, for the banking application used throughout this book, would be to provide a way to execute your unit tests using nosetest. Create the `pavement.py` file and add that task now:

```
from paver.tasks import task
from paver.easy import sh
```

```
@task
def unit_tests():
    sh('nosetests test/unit')
```

Notice how easy it is to define the task and defer to the command line that you already know how to use to execute your tests. Paver provides the convenient `sh` method to execute any command you wish as you would from the command line. You may also notice that Paver is just making use of standard Python code to define each task, so it is easy to customize each task and perform any function you may need to in your task.

Executing Paver Tasks

You can execute the task you have created simply by running the following at the command line:

```
$ paver unit_tests
---> pavement.unit_tests
nosetests test/unit
..
-----------------------------------------------
Ran 2 tests in 0.001s
OK
```

Paver uses the name of the method you defined as the task name. When you execute the task, Paver outputs the task it is running from the pavement file, which is of more use when running the default task or those that cause other tasks to be executed so that you get a full history of what Paver is actually running. You also get the output of the commands you are executing as if you were running them stand-alone, so you can see the preceding nosetest output as expected, showing it ran the two tests and both passed.

The output becomes more interesting and helpful when tests fail. Paver is able to capture tasks that produce a non-zero exit code (which indicates whether a command successfully executed) and report on what caused the failure. It also clearly states that something failed in the build and is easily picked up by Jenkins jobs, for example (see later in the chapter). There, it can mark the build as failed so that you can investigate the problem. If you cause a test to fail, you will see output similar to this:

```
$ paver unit_tests
---> pavement.unit_tests
nosetests test/unit
.F
================================================================
```

```
FAIL: test_add_account (test.unit.bank_test.BankTest)
-------------------------------------------------------------
Traceback (most recent call last):
  File "/Users/username/workspace/bank/test/unit/bank_test.py",
  line 18, in test_add_account
    self.assertEqual(len(bank.accounts), 500)
AssertionError: 2 != 500


-------------------------------------------------------------
Ran 2 tests in 0.001s

FAILED (failures=1)

Captured Task Output:
--------------------

---> pavement.unit_tests
nosetests test/unit
Build failed running pavement.unit_tests: Subprocess return code: 1
```

Paver outputs clearly which task caused the issue and, of course, the output from nosetest allows you to investigate which test failed so that you can fix the problem to get the build passing again.

Defining a Default Build

Now you know how to define a task in Paver. You can go ahead and add other tasks that form your default build process. As mentioned earlier, you need to execute Paver and have it run the unit and lettuce tests while providing code coverage results and finishing with the PyLint code analysis. You could define this set of tasks like so:

```python
from paver.tasks import task, BuildFailure
from paver.easy import sh

@task
def unit_tests():
    sh('nosetests --with-coverage test/unit')

@task
def lettuce_tests():
    sh('lettuce test/bdd')
```

```
@task
def run_pylint():
    try:
        sh('pylint --msg-template="{path}:{line}:
 [{msg_id}({symbol}), {obj}] {msg}" bank/ > pylint.txt')
    except BuildFailure:
        pass
```

This set of tasks provides a base build that you should run against every code check-in. Note how the PyLint task has been defined. It has been coded this way because PyLint returns a non-zero return code when it finds any PyLint errors. Therefore, unless you specifically want to fail your builds due to PyLint errors (which are not as serious as test failures) you need to capture the exception that Paver raises. You also need to output the PyLint results to a file so that the errors can be read in by a Jenkins plug-in later. You have to specify that the output be in the preceding format so that the Jenkins plug-in will be able to read the file and produce the correct graph. Previous versions of PyLint allowed for a format to be passed in as "parseable." However, this has now been deprecated and so must be replaced by the message format shown earlier. The plug-in will display a chart showing the PyLint errors, so that you can easily monitor the amount of errors from build to build.

Of course, if you were to run just Paver from the command line now, it would not know what to execute by default and indeed returns straightaway because it has no tasks to run. To get the behavior you want, you must define a default task and make use of the needs-decorator to create a dependency on the tasks to be executed, essentially before the default task that will be empty.

```
@needs('unit_tests', 'lettuce_tests', 'run_pylint')
@task
def default():
    pass
```

Now when you execute the paver command, it performs each of the tasks listed in the needs section in order, from unit_tests first through to run_pylint last. Paver output shows clearly which task it is running; it also neatly slices up your output so you can find the problem areas quicker.

```
$ paver
---> pavement.default
---> pavement.unit_tests
nosetests --with-coverage test/unit
..
```

```
Name              Stmts    Miss   Cover   Missing
--------------------------------------------------
bank                  1       0    100%
bank.account          4       0    100%
bank.bank             5       0    100%
--------------------------------------------------
TOTAL                10       0    100%
--------------------------------------------------
Ran 2 tests in 0.002s

OK
---> pavement.lettuce_tests
lettuce test/bdd

Feature: Bank web application to retrieve
         and update customer accounts
  # test/bdd/features/bank.feature:1
  As a customer I wish to be able to view my balance
  # test/bdd/features/bank.feature:3
  and update my balance
  # test/bdd/features/bank.feature:4
  and withdraw from my balance
  # test/bdd/features/bank.feature:5

1 feature (1 passed)
2 scenarios (2 passed)
8 steps (8 passed)
---> pavement.run_pylint
pylint bank/ > pylint.txt
```

Output from this example is shortened.

Setting Up Automated Builds

With the build tasks in place and an easy way to execute everything you need to check your code, you can now set up Jenkins to perform all these tasks for you on every commit. Developers know this setup as continuous integration. They use this name because as every developer checks in his or her changes to the code, the code is being "continuously integrated" into the existing code. Jenkins is set up to poll the repository for changes every minute; when it detects a change, it kicks off the job, which will run the build tasks to prove that none of the previously working behavior of the application has been broken. Another key part of this process is that it takes place (usually) on an external machine other than that which the developer writes the code on. This helps to prove that the code works on any environment and that the team has created the application in a way that it can download and install its dependencies without relying on a specific machine setup. This is where the use of the Python Pip tool is vital to manage your dependencies.

Installing Jenkins

Of course, to begin setting up your build, you must first install Jenkins on the machine you will designate to this task. You must also set up the machine with any system dependencies your project may have that cannot be installed from the code base, such as Python, gcc (to compile C code that some Python packages require), and any other required libraries. Once you have done this, it may be worth writing a script to automatically set up any machine with the required toolset. This may help to make it easy in the future, such as when a new developer joins your team or if you need to build the machine from scratch again.

Ideally, you would use a machine with a decent specification to handle the build process since you may run many jobs from one machine. At a minimum, use a machine similar to your development setup. If you are using a Linux distribution such as Ubuntu, you should be able to install Jenkins from the default package manager by running the following:

> Unfortunately, the Jenkins package is no longer in Ubuntu 14.04 and must be installed from upstream packages. Please consult the Jenkins website for up to date information regarding installation instructions for Ubuntu and other operating systems. You can also search Google for various discussion and solutions to the problem.

```
$ sudo apt-get install jenkins
```

If you are setting up a Mac OS X machine for your build, you should install the Brew package manager, as mentioned earlier in the book, and run the following from the command line:

```
$ brew install jenkins
```

Jenkins is a Java application and is installed as a war file to your machine. It should be started up as a daemon process upon installation and you can check if it is running by visiting its default location of `http://localhost:8080`. Should you find it isn't running, the following command for Linux should get you up and running:

```
$ /etc/init.d/jenkins start
```

For OS X, use this:

```
launchctl load ~/Library/LaunchAgents/homebrew.mxcl.jenkins.plist
```

To begin creating the build job, click the Create New Jobs link. (See Figure 10-1.) You will then be presented with some options about the type of job to create.

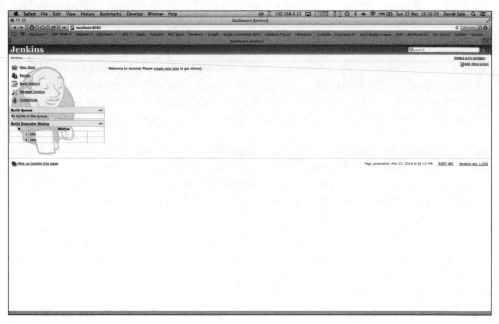

FIGURE 10-1: Jenkins interface upon first launch.

Here you want to choose Build a Free-style Software Project because this is the first build you will be making. (See Figure 10-2.) Later you may want to use Copy from Existing Job if you are making a similar build with only a few tweaks. Give the job a name that is relevant to the project and click OK to create your job.

You should now be presented with the configuration screen for the build job you have created. (See Figure 10-3.) Give the job a description if you'd like, and then move on to the Source Code Management section.

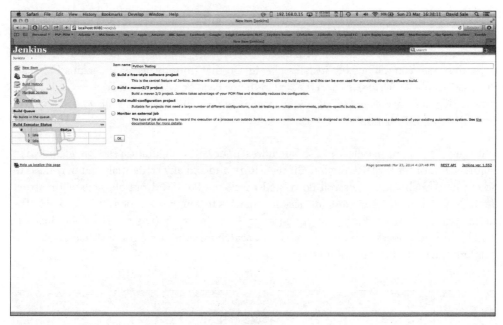

FIGURE 10-2: Name and create a free-style build job.

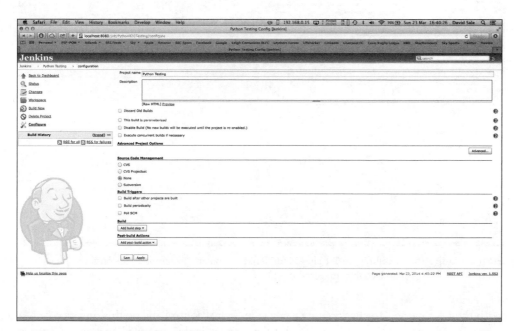

FIGURE 10-3: Configuring the build job in Jenkins.

This section will enable you to instruct Jenkins to monitor your source control for the project for any changes and kick off your build to give you the continuous integration you are looking to implement. Notice that by default Jenkins doesn't support Git. Should you require Git, as you do in this case, you will need to install a plug-in. Do that from the Manage Jenkins⇨Manage Plugins⇨Available Tab interface on the Jenkins home page. You can save this job for now, install the Git plug-in from the Jenkins plug-in management page, and then return to your build job to continue the configuration.

With the Git plug-in installed, you should now see the Git configuration section, as shown in Figure 10-4. Enter the URL of your Git repository and add any credentials you may need to access it. You should then scroll down and check the Poll SCM option. This will instruct Jenkins about how often it should check for changes to your source code. This is done in the same style as cron job configuration; entering * * * * * (five asterisks) will instruct Jenkins to check every minute. You can easily search for other time frames should you wish a different length than one minute.

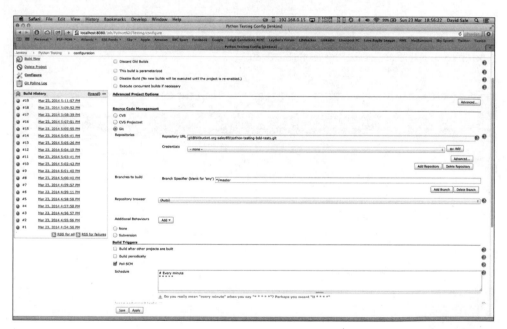

FIGURE 10-4: After installing the Git plug-in for Jenkins, you are presented with configuration options for Git as a source code management tool.

With the job now able to check out by using your source control and do this on any changes to the source code, all that remains is to configure what Jenkins should do when it detects a change. You are able to execute commands, just like you would on the command line of your own machine by choosing the Execute Shell option from the Add Build Step drop-down menu in the Build section. The build performs the following actions, in order:

1. Create a Python virtual environment to install the dependencies to and execute the build.

2. Activate the new virtual environment.

3. Use Pip to install the project dependencies.

4. Execute the default Paver task to run the entire build you have created.

To configure this in Jenkins, add two shells to be executed (see Figure 10-5). Splitting shells is a good idea; Jenkins will generally use the last command's exit code to determine whether a build has failed. In the first shell, add the following lines:

```
source ~/.profile
virtualenv ${WORKON_HOME}/jenkins-build --no-site-packages –
  distribute
```

Replace .profile with the relevant bash settings you have configured, such as .bashrc or .bash_profile. You are doing this here to source the line that gives the shell access to the virtualenv commands. The second line then creates the virtualenv that the build job will use in the standard location within the user's home folder.

In the second shell, add the following lines:

```
. ~/.virtualenvs/jenkins-build/bin/activate
pip install -r requirements.txt
paver
```

This shell activates the virtualenv you have just created, installs the application's dependencies, and then runs the Paver command to execute the build tasks you defined earlier. (See Figure 10-5.)

With the configuration complete, you can now click Save and you will be taken back to the main page for the job. If you click Build Now, Jenkins should check out your source code from Git and then work through each step of the job configuration. It will continue until it either fails at some point or completes successfully. Should the build fail for any reason, click Console Output. (See Figure 10-6.) There, you should be able to decipher where and why the build failed and correct the situation.

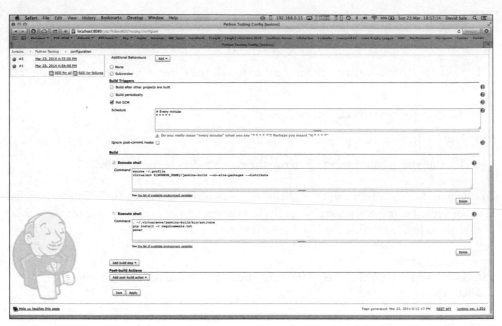

FIGURE 10-5: Execute shell configuration to create the virtualenv, install dependencies, and execute the build.

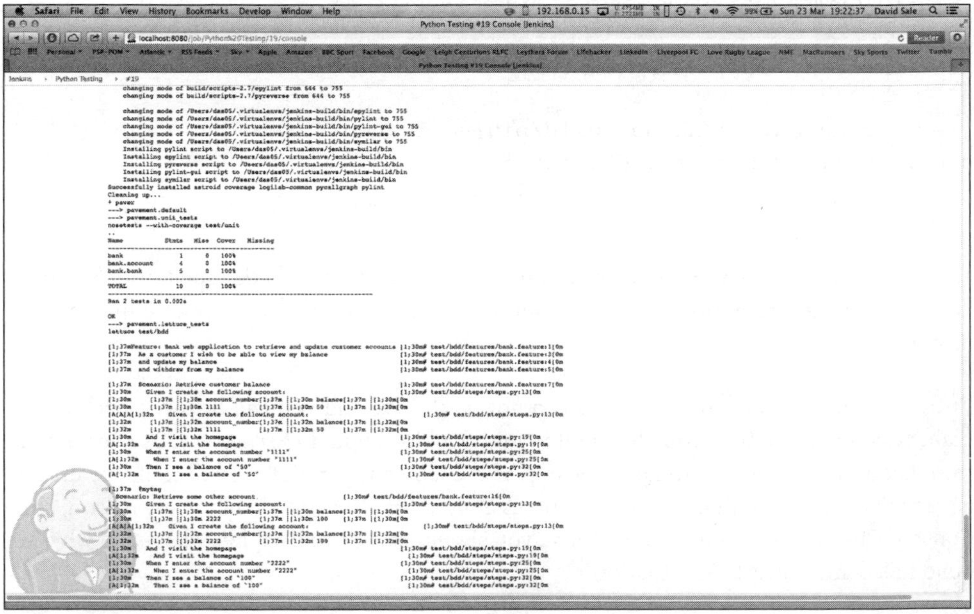

FIGURE 10-6: Console Output provides a view for your build jobs.

Adding Coverage and PyLint Reports

The only part missing from your continuous integration build is the reports that you can generate from the Paver tasks. Because you have coverage and PyLint running as part of your build, you are already set up to add the integration to Jenkins. Coverage is already outputting a file called `coverage.xml` that the Jenkins plug-in you will install will expect to pick up to produce the report. You have forced PyLint to output its results to a `pylint.txt` file, which again, the plug-in will read to produce the PyLint information chart.

Generating a PyLint Report

The plug-in you will need to install for PyLint first is known as Violations. This plug-in supports many kinds of code-checking tools, such as jslint and checkstyle. You should install the plug-in as you did for Git previously, and then go into the build job and click Configure. You can add then add the check for PyLint by adding a Post Build Action at the end of your configuration. (See Figure 10-7.) Choose Report Violations and Jenkins adds a list of different tools you can use to check your code. On the row that specifies PyLint, you need only to add the filename to the PyLint output you have generated. In this case add `pylint.txt`. You can then optionally alter the numbers shown to the left to mark the build as unstable after the PyLint errors reach a certain amount. It is up to you, however, if you want to use this feature. With the configuration in place, upon a completed build you will be presented a graph tracking the amount of PyLint errors from each build on the job's homepage. (See Figure 10-8.)

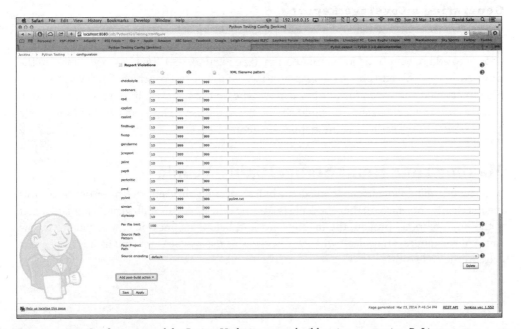

FIGURE 10-7: Configuration of the Report Violations post build action to monitor PyLint errors.

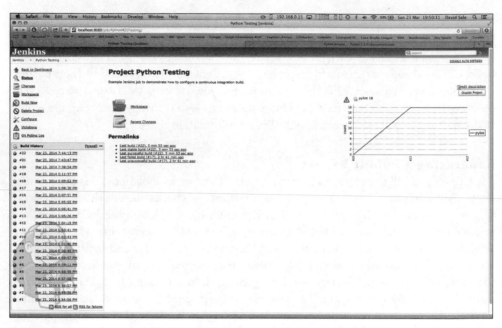

FIGURE 10-8: Graph produced by Report Violations to track the number of PyLint errors in each build.

Generating a Coverage Report

Coverage reporting requires the Cobertura plug-in to be installed in the same way the preceding Jenkins plug-ins are installed. Again, this will enable a Post Build Action that you can choose to add to your build job configuration. (See Figure 10-9.) The plug-in will pick up the `coverage.xml` file and create the graph to track your unit test coverage. Once you have the plug-in enabled and added to your job, simply type `coverage.xml` in the box presented to you and run the build again. The build should parse the `coverage.xml` file and produce a graph similar to the earlier PyLint graph. (See Figure 10-10.)

Making Your Build Status Highly Visible

Automated builds allow teams to make the build status highly visible to the entire team. This means clearly showing whether the build is passing or failing. This high visibility ensures that if the build becomes broken, the failure is noticed before anyone adds more code to it. The cause of the failure can be dealt with swiftly, and this means you catch and fix any issues that arise in the code early.

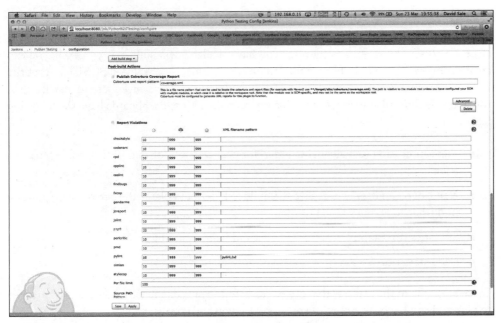

FIGURE 10-9: Configuration of the Cobertura plug-in post build action, which produces unit test coverage reports.

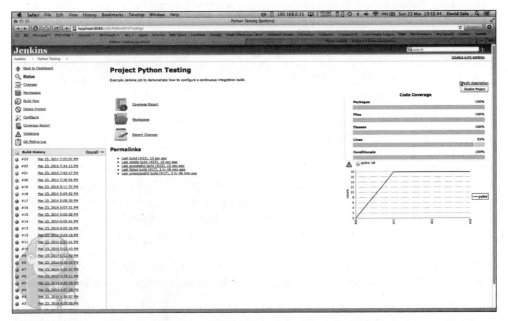

FIGURE 10-10: Chart produced by the Cobertura plug-in tracking overall unit test coverage for your application.

Making your build status highly visible usually involves creating some sort of dashboard that is large and clear enough to be seen by the entire team. Ideally, this would be displayed on a large TV screen; however, any monitor you have available will suffice. If you wish, you can create your own custom dashboard for Jenkins by making use of the API provided to get the information and display as you choose. Most people/teams, however, choose to install one of the many Jenkins plug-ins that offer this functionality. Most dashboards have the following features:

- Clear indication (usually using green for pass and red for fail) of the build status for a job

- Name of committer who caused the build to fail (not to blame the person but to quickly find what code caused the failed build)

- Statistics (for example, number of jobs and failing/passing builds)

- Code statistics (for example, coverage and PyLint reports)

These are some of the features that are typically found on a dashboard; however, you are free to pick and choose what is required or useful for you and your team.

A quick search on the plug-ins directory within the Jenkins management options will show you that there are many off-the-shelf solutions for the dashboard. A few are particularly worth mentioning, including one that includes a setup walk-through.

- eXtreme Feedback Panel: `https://wiki.jenkins-ci.org/display/JENKINS/eXtreme+Feedback+Panel+Plugin`

- Radiator View Plugin: `https://wiki.jenkins-ci.org/display/JENKINS/Radiator+View+Plugin`

- Build Monitor Plugin: `https://wiki.jenkins-ci.org/display/JENKINS/Build+Monitor+Plugin`

All three do the job adequately, but the one you should focus on here is the eXtreme Feedback Panel. As mentioned previously, click Manage Jenkins⟹Manage Plugins⟹Available and then search for the plug-in. Once you find it, select the check box next to it and click Download Now and Install after Restart. When the plug-in has downloaded, visit `http://localhost:8080/restart` (or wherever your Jenkins is hosted) and click Yes to restart.

With the plug-in installed, you now create the Build Monitor and add the jobs you want to display to it. On your Jenkins homepage, click the little plus symbol (+) next to the word All above your list of jobs. This will bring up the "Add View" page where you can type the view name in the View Name box and select the eXtreme Feedback Panel option. (See Figure 10-11.)

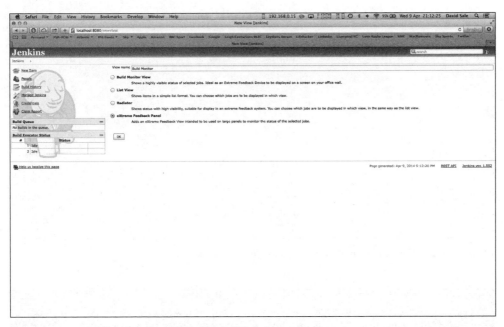

FIGURE 10-11: Adding the eXtreme Feedback Panel view to Jenkins.

After creating the view, you will be presented with the configuration options for the build monitor. (See Figure 10-12.) Select the job(s) you want to monitor, and then configure the view as you prefer, selecting what order to display the jobs in (this option is visible in Figure 10-12), colors to use to indicate different statuses, and how many to display per row and column (found lower down on the page in Figure 10-12).

With the configuration complete, all that is left is to click Save and you will be presented with the Build Monitor status. (See Figure 10-13.) The monitor refreshes every 3 seconds to get the latest build status for the jobs selected. Simply display this somewhere visible to the team to keep your builds in check.

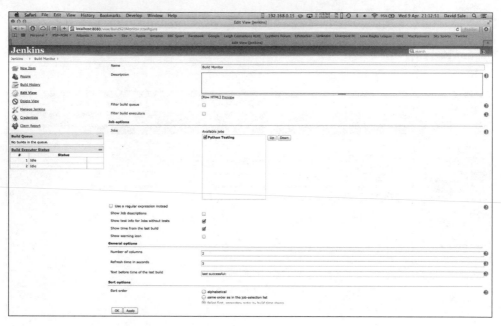

FIGURE 10-12: Configuration options for the eXtreme Feedback Panel.

FIGURE 10-13: eXtreme Feedback Panel configured to monitor a single job.

Summary

This chapter focused on taking your toolset to the next level and provided great ways to automate your entire testing processes. A continuous integration build is a must in today's development practices and ensures you check every facet of your application on every code check-in. By removing the possibility of human error in the checks that are being made, you ensure that every build of your code is going through identical checks, giving you confidence in the artifact to be released.

You were introduced to the task management library Paver, which enables you to leverage Python code and bash execution to help automate your daily testing commands. By creating a default task, Paver enables you to define all the individual elements of your testing suite and execute them all in one easy command. Because it is using only Python code underneath, it is unnecessary to customize tasks to suit project's needs for defining a full build process.

Following on from Paver, Jenkins was used to actually check the tasks on every check-in of code. With such a large community working to improve and add more features to Jenkins, it is a great tool to choose for running your build. It has great support whenever you encounter any issues, usually finding answers to your problems within the first few clicks of a Google search. It also provides a huge library of plug-ins to support anything you may need, as shown in the coverage and Lint plug-ins used in this chapter.

Resources

Paver: `http://paver.github.io/paver/`

Jenkins: `http://jenkins-ci.org`

Coverage: `http://nedbatchelder.com/code/coverage/`

PyLint: `http://www.pylint.org`

Jenkins Cobertura Plugin: `https://wiki.jenkins-ci.org/display/JENKINS/Cobertura+Plugin`

Jenkins Violations Plugin: `https://wiki.jenkins-ci.org/display/JENKINS/Violations`

Jenkins Plugins: `https://wiki.jenkins-ci.org/display/JENKINS/Plugins`

Chapter 11
Deploying Your Application

YOUR END GOAL is actually releasing the product you built to your customers. The example applications discussed so far have been small and self-contained and therefore after thorough unit and behavior testing would be ready to be "released" straightaway with not much further testing. However, what if the applications you are building are small components that form a larger application stack? For example, the data handling and processing might reside on back-end components and some other components collect this data and display the front end to the customer. In such a scenario, your code might pass through many iterations before you have the confidence to release it to customers. Essentially, you should put into place a deployment pipeline, and as the code moves through the pipeline your confidence in the business readiness of the various features or product changes can only grow.

The chapter looks at how you can construct such a pipeline and the kinds of tests and tooling you can build around components to ensure that you have integrated them successfully with the rest of stack before releasing to your customers.

The key aspects of this chapter include deployment to various environments, such as the development, stage deployment, and production. The different environments provide isolated or integrated areas for your components to enable QAs and developers to test their applications as required.

Another notable area of the chapter is that of writing automated smoke tests, which give you the capability to run repeatable tests that check whether the components are working together (called integration tests). This type of testing is crucial for ensuring the application stack you are deploying into a production environment will work together and deliver on the functionality that your customers expect. Smoke testing in this way also gives you the opportunity to fix any issues in your components that are causing integration issues before they are released to customers.

Finally, this chapter walks you through the release process for your applications and shows how to make it as easy and reusable as possible. How can you release seamlessly so that your customers never even know the application has changed? Can you release every month, week, day, or even hour? Making releases easy, simple, and frequent makes your life as a developer easier. This chapter looks at how you can work toward that goal.

Deploying Your Application to Production

Because deploying to production introduces a risk to your business or application, it is sensible to minimize that risk and maximize your confidence in your deployment. On the other hand, because each deployment should be adding business value to your application it is likely you want to deliver these features as quickly and as often as possible. This means that you have time pressures to contend with, while also striving to deliver a high-quality product and zero defects on every release. This sounds like conflicting requirements, right? However, it is possible to streamline your deployment processes to get the speed of delivery you want while ensuring that the quality of your product remains high.

Everything described in this book so far has been the part of the building blocks for this deployment pipeline, depicted in Figure 11-1, which starts the moment a requirement is brought to the development team through code and tests. The process can be summarized in the following stages.

1. Development team writes code, unit tests, and possibly some of the acceptance tests.

2. QAs check for defects and write more acceptance tests.

3. Application is deployed to test environments.

4. Application undergoes performance and integration testing on deployed environments.

5. Application is promoted to stage (preproduction) environment.

6. Smoke tests are run against the stage environment to ensure components work together correctly. (See later in this chapter for more details.)

7. Application is deployed to production environment.

Feature delivery to production marks the end of the process. Deployment is the final stage in the life cycle of delivery; when you break delivery into frequent, bite-sized chunks, your customers get to see new features more quickly. Small isolated deployments give you control over the delivery of your product.

FIGURE 11-1: The deployment pipeline includes multiple testing and deployment stages.

Many options for deploying an application to an environment are available. Where or what you deploy to essentially boils down to factors surrounding your application, which can include the following:

- The language the application is written in

- Cost of environment/deployment location

- Security concerns (for example, deploying to an internal network to limit access from the outside world to sensitive data)

- Legacy or compatibility issues that force an application to be deployed in a certain way

With these factors in mind, you have numerous options for deploying your application—such as established server deployments made up of physical machines and virtual machines. These can be in-house or you can purchase the use of servers on many websites across the Internet. More recently, there has been a large movement toward cloud-based deployment of applications, providing flexible and expandable models for hosting your application. This is known in the industry as Platform as a Service (PaaS). The cloud offers huge benefits in terms of being able to scale your application up or down instantly when it receives more traffic, for example. Many providers offer web-based cloud platforms and among the more famous are, Google App Engine, Heroku, and EngineYard. Later in the chapter, you can find an example using Heroku, which is used to host my portfolio website written in Python's Django web framework.

Creating a Deployable Artifact

As part of the deployment pipeline, you must put your application somewhere but what exactly do you deploy? How do you instruct the system that the application is going to be installed on what to install? What files are part of the package you need to create? How do you manage your application's dependencies? In this section, you dive into creating a deployable artifact that contains everything required to install and run your application. The artifact must be created at the end of every successful build and be tagged in some way so that you can choose an artifact that you know is completely tested, contains all the required changes and features you need for a release, and deploy it across the environments up to production as required. Crucially, by having such an artifact, you know that the code is *exactly* the same every time you deploy it. This helps to eliminate inconsistencies within the code and avoid confusing and seemingly random behavior as you move to production.

Defining the Paver Tasks

To create the deployable artifact, you need to make some additions to the paver tasks you defined earlier. Previously, you used paver just to execute your different test suites as part of a build. Now you are going to add some standard packaging commands to create the setup script and package containing all your code as required. The code to be added to the `pavement.py` file is as follows:

```
from paver.setuputils import setup, find_package_data

package_data = find_package_data()
entry_points = {
    'console_scripts': [
        'run_server = bank.bank_app:main',
        ]
}

setup(name='bank_app',
      version='0.0.1',
      author='David Sale',
      maintainer='David Sale',
      description='Example application to demonstrate
                   Python testing techniques.',
      license='License :: Public Domain',
      include_package_data=True,
      packages=['bank'],
      package_data=package_data,
      entry_points=entry_points)

@task
@needs('paver.misctasks.generate_setup',
       'distutils.command.sdist')
def sdist():
    """Generates the setup file and packages up the
  commercial_inventory application."""
```

This code specifies the contents of the package to be created. Python's included library `setuputils` provides a handy method for recursively grabbing the files that need to be included using `find_package_data()`. Then the code defines how to start the application from the command line after the package is installed. This example uses the command `run_server` and links to the method in the code that actually starts up the development server for the application. Therefore, if you look at the code you have specified as the entry point, it is actually executing the main method in `bank_app`.

```
from flask import Flask, render_template, request
from bank import Bank
from account import Account
```

```
app = Flask(__name__)
BANK = Bank()

@app.route('/')
def hello_world():
    account_number = request.args.get('account_number')
    balance = BANK.get_account_balance(account_number)
    return render_template('index.html', balance=balance)


def main():
    account = Account('1111', 50) #pylint: disable=C0103
    BANK.add_account(account)
    app.run(debug=True)

if __name__ == '__main__':
    main()
```

Finally, the `sdist` task that is defined in the `pavement.py` file is used to generate your `setup.py` file, using the `setuptools` and `distutils` library to create it. It is standard for Python packages to provide a `setup.py` file that can be installed from in the usual manner of `python setup.py install`.

Incorporating Packaging into the Build

With this code in place in the `pavement.py` file, you are now able to build this packaging of the app into your build process, which can be run on Jenkins. Jenkins can also be configured to archive your deployable artifact, which essentially gives you a link between the code and that build number. When you have a build that passes tests and contains all the features you want to release, you can take the build artifact from that build and deploy the code that was packaged.

To add the packaging of the app to the build, you simply need to add the new task to the default task, which runs when you execute `paver` from the command line. It would be logical to add the packaging of the app as the last item of the build, so that if the test fails you don't create a package unnecessarily. If the tests for a build have failed, you are unlikely to ever want to deploy that code anyway. Add the `sdist` task to the `default` needs section and then run `paver` again to see that at the end of the build it does indeed build the package.

```
@needs('unit_tests', 'lettuce_tests', 'run_pylint', 'sdist')
@task
def default():
    pass
```

Enabling Archiving on Jenkins

Jenkins provides a way to specify the location that your build will output a deployable artifact to and can automatically archive this artifact for you as part of the build. From the work to add the task to the default build, you should now be able to see that the `sdist` task creates a `dist` folder that stores the tarball package of your entire application. This is the file you want to archive and is the path you need to specify within the Jenkins job configuration. Open the configuration for your build job in Jenkins and scroll down to the bottom. You should see the Add Post-Build Action option. Within the drop-down, choose Archive the Artifacts and then enter the following path for Jenkins to look where to get the artifact from. (See Figure 11-2.)

```
dist/bank_app-0.0.1.tar.gz
```

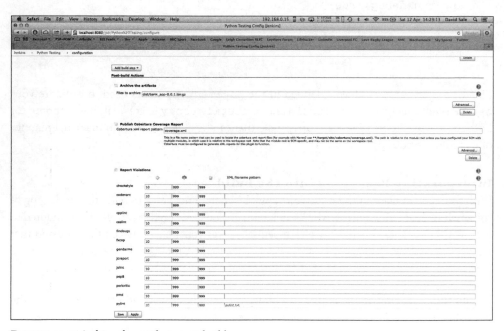

FIGURE 11-2: Archive the artifacts post-build.

After filling in the path, click Save and run the build. If everything is working after the build, you should be able to see the artifact has been archived by viewing the build job overview page. That page should now contain a link to the archive. You can see an example of this in Figure 11-3.

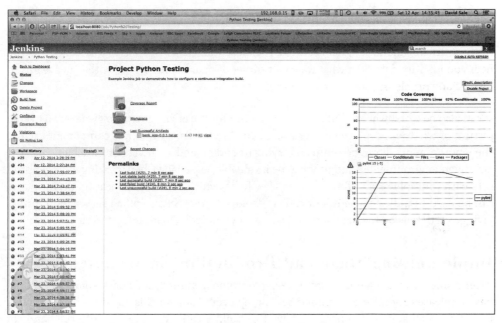

FIGURE 11-3: The archived artifact is displayed in the build job overview page.

With the archive now in place, you can set up a deployment process as you want. You could create some Jenkins jobs that download the artifact, untar it, and deploy it to the environment you want to use to host your application. Numerous options are available here. Just decide what works best for your setup.

QA Environment

When deployments and environments are discussed in the software development communities, numerous environments are commonly used to deploy an application. The environments serve different purposes before reaching production. One of these environments is generally a QA or test environment. This is the first time the code is deployed to an environment after the code has been developed on a developer's local machine. As the application is deployed it can be tested by other people (such as QAs) on a realistic environment as if the application were running for real. You can also perform other types of testing at this stage, such as integration testing to see how the application functions with other components in the stack or performance testing to see how well the application will cope with the type of load it is expected to encounter in production.

Depending on how many teams or other components depend on the application you are building, you should set up multiple QA environments so that you can deploy the code as needed by the external dependents on your application. This way they can test and verify that the functionality you built is working as expected. You should aim to deploy frequently to these environments, so that everyone is exposed to the latest code as it is built. This will help you identify defects in what was built earlier or enable you to work with other teams to resolve any problems your changes caused.

It can also be worthwhile to build a status monitor for the environment to give you an overall picture of what was deployed where and when. As you deploy multiple components across the environments, it can be confusing trying to understand what versions are being used in any given environment. A monitor can be invaluable, especially when working in larger projects with multiple teams. Tools such as New Relic, which monitor application performance can be used to indicate where your code is deployed. The tool also offers server monitoring, giving you details on the hardware and status of your deployment infrastructure.

Implementing Stage and Production Environments

After numerous testing hurdles have been overcome, you reach the point where you should have a release candidate or the build containing everything for this release, which has been tested from all angles. You need to move this build into production and into the hands of customers who want the new features, but you also want some control. What if something unforeseen happens (for example, your code goes live but stops sales on your website)? How can you quickly fix the problem without your customers noticing? This is where the stage environment comes in, along with the concepts of online and offline coupled with load balancers.

The stage environment is an exact replica of your production environment. This means the hardware, number of application instances running, and network configuration all should be identical to your production environment. This identical setup lets you deploy your code on stage and see how it will behave in a production deployment. This safety net deployment should help you catch simple but harmful mistakes, such as firewall misconfiguration or too few instances to handle load, which would cause a bad experience for your application customers.

Online and offline legs provide another element of control that you can apply during your release process. You basically set up an environment so that the traffic has two ways to go. For example, if your website has a domain of `http://mysite.com`, the traffic hitting that domain will always be routed to the online, or live, leg. Meanwhile, while gearing up for a release, you could deploy to the offline leg, which has a domain of `http://mysite-offline.com`. This domain, depicted in Figure 11-4, will only route traffic to the offline leg and allows you to quickly check or even smoke test your application to ensure it is working correctly.

You can then perform a cutover that switches the legs so that your new release becomes the online leg and receives the traffic from `http://mysite.com` and vice versa. This idea also stretches to any persistence layer you may have in your application stack. For example in the stage environment you would want to mirror your production database. This would be done at least in terms of setup and structure but using test data to avoid the misuse of real customer data. Similarly for online and offline legs, each application would have its own copy of the database, keeping the two environments isolated.

Doing this offers two key advantages. One is the capability to test your application before going live to customers, but also, if problems do arise, you can quickly cutover to return to the previous working version of the code while you work on a fix. Due to the testing the code has gone through from the start, this should be a rare occurrence—but at least the capability is there should the worst happen.

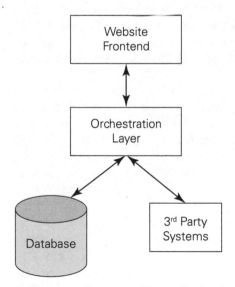

FIGURE 11-4: Designing offline and online legs for an application lets you test new code without committing to it, because you can always switch legs.

Implementing a Cloud Deployment

One of the biggest movements in recent years in the deployment space has been toward utilizing the flexibility and scalability of the cloud. The cloud is a term used to describe a collection of multiple pieces of hardware that to the end user is just one large resource they can make use of. So you could setup a cloud with 5 servers each providing 1TB hard drive and 8GB of RAM. Users of the cloud will simply see there is 5TB of hard drive space and 40GB of RAM.

The user can then allocate a partition of these resources to their application. Often the clouds used by enterprise organizations are scaled massively and can provided immense amounts of resources for their development estate to make use of.

Whilst still considered to be something of a buzzword in computing, more and more enterprises and services move to the cloud as it is starting to be regarded as the standard way to deploy. Cloud deployment can make a great deal of sense from a financial point of view, because many cloud platforms offer pay-as-you-use plans where you are charged by usage, CPU time, or a collection of metrics to calculate a monthly cost. This can often be more cost effective than hiring or maintaining a set of physical hardware servers within your company.

The cloud allows you, as a developer, to have more control over your application's behavior and performance moving away from a centralized Development Operations team. The cloud supports scaling up and down the instances and memory available to your application. Say you have just run an ad on TV that directs people to your website. You are likely to see a sudden spike in the traffic. With the cloud, you can double your instances to cope with the increased load and then scale it back down after traffic subsides. Some cloud platforms even provide this as an automated service, with the scaling handled for you so you never need to worry.

One of the popular choices for cloud deployment is Heroku. First and foremost, it offers you the capability to host an application for free if you can cope with having only one *dyno* (a lightweight container running a single user-specified command), which should be enough for a relatively simple website. You also get 10,000 rows of a Postgres database for free too. Essentially, Heroku provides a great place for you to try out cloud deployment before committing to it as your production solution.

Heroku simplifies the process of setting up an account and deploying your application. Heroku leverages Git, the source code management tool to push your codebase to Heroku's servers and provide a `Procfile` that instructs Heroku how to start up your application. The process is best explained by looking at an example. My website is hosted on Heroku; you can find it at `www.dsale.co.uk`.

Creating a Heroku Account

The first step before being able to deploy to Heroku is to create your account. Simply visit `www.heroku.com` and follow the instructions to set up your account. Once your account is up and running, head to Apps and click Create App. Give your app a name and click Create. You will then be provided with a domain for your application and, importantly, a Git repository URL. With your app created, you need to install the Heroku tool belt for your system, which will provide you with the Heroku command line tools to enable the deployment. You can find the tool belt at `https://toolbelt.heroku.com`.

Creating a Small Application

For this example, you can use a skeleton Flask application to test that you can set everything up correctly and get the app running on Heroku. You can then build on this skeleton to create your website, for example. Add the following code to a file named `python_testing.py` in a directory on your system somewhere:

```python
from flask import Flask

app = Flask(__name__)


@app.route('/')
def hello_world():
    return 'Hello World!'


if __name__ == '__main__':
    app.run()
```

Run `python_testing.py` application locally and visit `http://localhost:5000` to see the words "Hello World!"

Setting up Git for Heroku

From the command line, change the directory to your application. Also, because it is not already under Git source control, perform the following steps:

```
$ cd myapp
$ git init
Initialized empty Git repository in .git/
$ git add .
$ git commit -m "my first commit"
Created initial commit 5df2d09: my first commit
 44 files changed, 8393 insertions(+), 0 deletions(-)
...
$ heroku git:remote -a NAME_OF_YOUR_APP_ON_HEROKU
Git remote heroku added.
```

Otherwise you could simply add the Heroku repo as a new remote, like so:

```
$ heroku git:remote -a NAME_OF_YOUR_APP_ON_HEROKU
Git remote heroku added.
```

Deploying the Application to Heroku

Now the application is set up to be pushed to Heroku; however, it is not quite ready to actually function on Heroku. You need to install a production-ready server for Python, such as Gunicorn, and add a `Procfile` to instruct Heroku how to start the server. To install Gunicorn, simply add a `requirements.txt` (which Heroku will look for to install the dependencies when it is pushed up) with `gunicorn==18.0` and `Flask==0.10.1`. With the dependencies handled, you can now add the Procfile at the root level of your project, with the following contents:

```
web: gunicorn python_testing:app
```

With all the files in place, you should have a structure that looks like this:

```
python-testing-dsale/
  python_testing.py
  requirements.txt
  Procfile
```

Now you just need to add those files to Git:

```
$ git add .
```

Commit locally:

```
$ git commit -m "Adding all code for release to Heroku."
[master c5c5256] Adding all code for release to Heroku


 2 files changed, 5 insertions(+), 5 deletions(-).
```

Then push the code up to Heroku.

```
$ git push heroku master
Fetching repository, done.
Counting objects: 9, done.
Delta compression using up to 8 threads.
Compressing objects: 100% (4/4), done.
Writing objects: 100% (5/5), 497 bytes | 0 bytes/s, done.
Total 5 (delta 3), reused 0 (delta 0)

-----> Python app detected
-----> No runtime.txt provided; assuming python-2.7.6.
-----> Using Python runtime (python-2.7.6)
-----> Installing dependencies using Pip (1.5.4)
       Cleaning up...
```

```
-----> Discovering process types
       Procfile declares types -> web

-----> Compressing... done, 30.3MB
-----> Launching... done, v5
       http://python-testing-dsale.herokuapp.com/ deployed to
  Heroku
```

If everything goes well, you should see the output on the command line, as shown in Figure 11-5, when you visit the domain assigned to your Heroku app. Here's the code to add the files to Git:

```
To git@heroku.com:python-testing-dsale.git
   43cd51f..c5c5256  master -> master
```

FIGURE 11-5: Hello World! application running on Heroku.

Smoke Testing a Deployed Application

Ensuring that your application behaves as expected when deployed to an environment is an important process. You could perform these kinds of checks manually, by visiting the website or calling the service you have just deployed and checking the response. However, doing this manually every time you deploy is a tedious process that could cause you to miss vital checks that you need to do on your application. Setting up a smoke-test suite is a sensible undertaking and not that difficult. The idea is not to test that every different feature of your application is performing as expected. Unit and acceptance testing should have covered those aspects of your application. Smoke tests should check that some of the key functions of your application are working as expected and prove that any dependent components are working in combination correctly with yours.

Smoke tests can be flexible in their implementation, and you should leverage any test tools or processes that make it easy for you to write them. A common implementation is to make use of the acceptance test frameworks to make requests to prove that certain *journeys* (routes through your application) behave as expected. Choose some of the key aspects of your application and check those, because if there is some problem in those journeys you are likely to have issues elsewhere, too. Key journeys also likely form part of your application core so if they are failing you will want a fix before going live. It is important to use smoke tests on your offline leg to test a release before going live. This strategy gives you a chance to fix issues before they go into production. You can then also run the smoke tests after a cutover makes your release live to give you confidence that the live components are indeed communicating correctly. This means you have a two-stage check to make sure everything is still okay after the cutover, and is not strictly needed but more of a sanity check that your deployment is successful.

Example Application Stack

To provide some context to smoke testing, it is worthwhile looking at an example application stack and the kinds of tests you could write for this type of situation. Many websites make use of multiple component architecture rather than relying on one heavyweight application. The multiple components work together to produce the end result displayed on the website. Earlier in the book, you looked at a small bank account application. If you wanted to put a website out to allow customers to check their accounts, you could split this application into multiple components (see Figure 11-6). You could envisage something along the lines of the following:

- **Web Application Frontend:** Website onto which customers would log in to view account details. Would make calls to underlying system for data and present on the page.

- **Orchestration Layer:** Application to handle making calls to other systems, such as payment handling, database queries to retrieve accounts, and so forth.

- **Database or Other 3rd Party systems:** Backend data layers that contain the account details and handle other functions or provide data that may not be held within this stack.

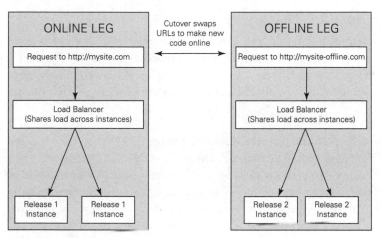

FIGURE 11-6: Architecture for example bank application website.

At the very least, you have three components in play for this type of application stack. This means the smoke tests you write for this application need to ensure that all components are covered by the calls you are making.

Smoke Test Scenarios

There would likely be a few scenarios you would want to check with a smoke test, such as having an account you can always log into, perhaps even on the production environments, to see that you can access the correct data. Following are examples of some of the scenarios you would likely cover with a smoke test.

- A customer can log in with the correct credentials and is shown the correct balance on the page.

- A customer attempts to log in with the wrong credentials and is shown an error page.

- A customer can withdraw from her account and the balance is updated.

- A 200 OK status code is returned when HTTP GET call made to all the components involved.

If all these tests are passing when you run them against one of your deployed environments, you can be fairly confident that your application is behaving correctly and the components are able to communicate to each other successfully.

Implementing Smoke Tests

You are free to use any implementation you like for the smoke tests; however, a good choice would be the Lettuce framework utilized for the Acceptance Testing in Chapters 7 and 8. Without the applications to call these tests on, examples of how you might code smoke tests are provided here and you should adapt these examples to the components you are working on.

The simplest checks you can perform in smoke tests result in the 200 OK status code being returned by some HTTP request to your application. The status code could be returned when making a GET call to the home page of the website or some status page you have hosted as part of the application on /about or /status. These kinds of pages can be useful for displaying deployment or building information about the version that is deployed. An about or status page also provides a quick check that your application is up and responding to requests. Say you have defined a status page within the application. You could write the following tests to run against your deployed environment:

```
Feature: Bank Application Smoke Tests

  As a developer I wish to check that all components are up
  and responding correctly to requests
  and providing the correct data

  Scenario: Make GET request to Frontend
    Given I make a GET request to http://frontend.com
    Then I receive a successful response
```

The steps behind the feature file could be implemented as follows:

```
@step(u'I make a GET request to "([^"]*)"')
def given_i_make_a_get_request_to(step, url):
    world.response = requests.get(url)
    print world.response

@step(u'I receive a successful response')
def then_i_receive_a_successful_response(step):
    assert_equal(world.response.status_code, 200)
```

Because the GET request step takes in the URL as a parameter, it is easy to switch the test to check any URL or environment you want to use. These quick tests allow you to run just one command to see if all your deployed components are running okay. The next tests to implement should check some business value, as described earlier. Take the scenario in which a customer can log in and check her balance. Again, a scenario definition for this type of test could be:

```
Scenario: Customer logs in and views balance
Given I visit the homepage
And enter username "david"
And enter password "12345"
And I click login
Then I see a balance of "50"
```

As you are making use of the Lettuce framework used earlier, you can also reuse some of the steps you have written within your smoke tests. By doing this, you minimize the amount of code you have to write for your smoke tests. This gives you the following set of steps to back up these tests:

```
@step(u'I visit the homepage')
def i_visit_the_homepage(step):
    world.browser = TestApp(app)
    world.response = world.browser.get('http://localhost:5000/')
    # here you could use configuration or environment variables
    # to sub in correct URL for the environment you wish to test.
    assert_equal(world.response.status_code, 200)

@step(u'And enter username "([^"]*)"')
def and_enter_username_group1(step, username):
    form = world.response.forms['account-form']
    form['username'] = username

@step(u'And enter password "([^"]*)"')
def and_enter_password_group1(step, password):
    form = world.response.forms['account-form']
    form['password'] = password

@step(u'I click login')
def and_i_click_login(step):
    world.response.click()

@step(u'I see a balance of "([^"]*)"')
def i_see_a_balance_of_group1(step, expected_balance):
    assert_in("Balance: {}".format(expected_balance),
  world.form_response.text)
```

It's then simply a case of building up as many journeys as you would like to cover with smoke tests. It is wise to make them as easy as possible to change the environment they are pointed at. Because you may be deploying to many different environments, you want to be able to make a one-line change to point the smoke tests at a different environment. This can be achieved in a few different ways, such as defining the base URL in a feature-scoped variable in the scenario background.

```
Given the base url is http://environment-1.com

@step(u'the base url is "([^"]*)"')
def the_base_url_is(step, base_url):
    world.base_url = base_url
```

You could also look up the URL from an environment variable and default it to your locally running version if not set. Then when you run against a certain environment, just set the environment variable to the URL you want to test.

```
$ export BASE_URL=http://environment-1.com

@step(u'I visit the homepage')
def i_visit_the_homepage(step):
    world.browser = TestApp(app)
    world.response = world.browser.get(os.environ.get('BASE_URL',
                    'http://localhost:5000'))
    assert_equal(world.response.status_code, 200)
```

The smoke tests should be checked in alongside your other test code within your projects and built into your build and deployment processes. For instance, if you use Jenkins to automate your deployments you could add the smoke tests as a final part of the deployment, which will either fail the build or pass, depending on the smoke test outcome.

Summary

This chapter introduced the process of deploying your application and how you can maintain complete control over the delivery of your product to customers. You saw established deployment processes, such as multiple environments for testing your application in different ways alongside offline and online legs. This ensures you put your code live to customers with maximum confidence in the product and minimum disruption to its availability.

With the rise of cloud deployment solutions and Platform as a Service (PaaS) offerings, the ease and flexibility of deploying to the cloud and the advantages this brings to your development process were discussed. The capability to easily scale your application up or down is a powerful tool that means you can cope with expanding traffic demands on your application instantly. The cloud also provides cost benefits with the capability to pay as you go, dependent on factors such as CPU time or number of instances running. However, regardless of where you deploy to, the structures and processes discussed in the chapter can be applied to any style of deployment, including in-house physical and virtual servers, rented servers, and the cloud. By building a stable, reliable deployment process and moving your code through the stages of a deployment pipeline, you will always deliver code confidently to customers. At the same time, the cutover fail-safe provides the capability to fix things quickly if something goes wrong.

Smoke testing provided another level of cover to the already extensive testing suite you have built up with unit, acceptance, and performance testing. You were shown how to create reusable tests that can be pointed at any environment you deploy to. The tests give you the capability to quickly check that an application has deployed correctly and is in a working state. Smoke tests add another layer to the feedback loop, notifying you quickly if there is an issue with your application after a deployment so that you can cut over again and fix the issue while your customers get uninterrupted, 100-percent available service.

By leveraging testing tools that you are already familiar with, you make the overhead of writing smoke tests minimal. They should focus only on some of the core elements of your application to ensure it is working correctly thereby reducing the number of tests that need to be written. The benefits of having automated tests over manually checking your applications after a deployment is the nature of their repetition. Manually checking is fine, but you may miss one of the checks you usually make—and it could be the breaking check. By having the smoke tests written and reused every time, you ensure the same checks are performed every time you release so that you catch any errors on the core journeys straightaway.

Resources

Heroku: `http://heroku.com`

Amazon EC2: `http://aws.amazon.com/ec2/`

Google App Engine: `https://appengine.google.com/`

Engine Yard: `https://www.engineyard.com`

Chapter 12
The Future of Testing Python

THIS FINAL CHAPTER of the book looks at what's next in terms of testing. As you have probably realized, many solutions are available for all kinds of testing problems. The testing scene in Python has advanced over the years and acted upon many of the developments that have happened in other languages. The Lettuce testing framework is a prime example of the Python community providing support for a great advancement in testing techniques, following the example set by Cucumber in the Ruby community. As you look beyond what is currently available or covered in this book, you will find numerous stories and articles about new ways of testing or handling code deployment. Most of the discussions seem to center around pushing the boundaries of what are currently considered the standard approaches. With advancement in computing power and the availability of the cloud becoming easier and easier, the types of testing, automation, and deployments that teams are able to build are becoming ever more complex. This chapter looks at what some of those advancements bring and how companies are implementing changes that are ultimately and massively beneficial to the products and services they deliver.

Stub the Solution

One of the more interesting testing techniques that has arisen recently is the capability to record and replay HTTP requests and sessions. Stub Servers, which are basically servers returning a static response based on some request input, have existed for a while. Incorporating these into your testing strategy allows you to make calls as if you were calling a real service and get an appropriate response back to use within your application. By making the calls over HTTP to a Stub Server you can test how your application will behave using a real network connection, but without actually calling the real service. This provides isolation from the other service which can prove important when performance testing, or in narrowing down a problem to a specific component or service.

Stubbing services in this way allows for much easier parallel working with other teams. Say, for example, your application is going to be calling a service developed by another team in your company. Previously, the service would have been defined on a whiteboard perhaps, and then sent around on a few e-mails with an expected request and response. With a stub, a real request and response can be defined and actually called by the application that is being developed against it. As the two teams work on their solutions, if something changes the stub can be updated, and if the changes break anything they can be dealt with straightaway. When the real service is built, you should be able to swap out the call to the stub for the real service and it should work as expected. (See Figure 12-1.)

FIGURE 12-1: VCR.py GitHub offering documentation and examples.

While manually creating the request and response in new services works okay, when you have an established service that is perhaps maintained outside your team or company's control you may want to stub that service in testing. Keeping stubs up to date can be time consuming, generally requiring manual coding of the response to send back and some form of mapping to indicate what request should prompt the response. Recently, however, libraries have started to appear, allowing for recording and replaying of responses from the real services. Libraries such as VCR.py allow you to make requests and store the responses in Cassettes (which are essentially YAML files, which a is a type of data serialization similar to JSON). You can then call upon those Cassettes in a context manager or decorator when writing your test.

```
with vcr.use_cassette('fixtures/vcr_cassettes/synopsis.yaml'):
    response = urllib2.urlopen(
                'http://www.iana.org/domains/reserved').read()
    assert 'Example domains' in response


@vcr.use_cassette('fixtures/vcr_cassettes/synopsis.yaml'):
def test_iana():
    response = urllib2.urlopen(
                'http://www.iana.org/domains/reserved').read()
    assert 'Example domains' in response
```

This style of testing, especially within HTTP Restful service development, is likely to grow in popularity. As mentioned, it can help enable much better collaboration across teams working to deliver a multi-component application stack. Stubbing services in this way opens up new avenues for testing, especially when dealing with systems in which data constantly changes. Stubs allow you to define a remote response so you know how your application should respond and thus check your application's expected behavior better in the test scenarios you build. Consult the Resources section later in this chapter for links to additional material on this subject.

Making Deployment Natural

In many businesses around the world, it is currently commonplace to have development, quality assurance, and DevOps teams based within departments. These teams often work separately from each other, leading to multiple code handoffs between teams. Code will usually be developed, then handed over to quality assurance and finally passed to DevOps or other teams for deployment to production environments. Often, this process can take days, weeks, or months, depending on the app being developed and the company involved. This kind of process is becoming old hat, with many successful start-ups and established companies moving to a much faster, efficient, and collaborative process.

Netflix is the prime case in point when looking at 21st-century development and deployment mechanisms. While other companies' teams deploy to production every couple of weeks, Netflix deploys over 100 times a day. Netflix accomplishes this because it combines the personnel required to move from code development to deployment to production together into a single team. The single team develops, deploys, and maintains its own servers and is accountable when those servers fail. Another vital part of the Netflix operation: automating nearly everything.

The process works like this: First, a developer checks code into the source control. This kicks off a build in Jenkins, which automates all the testing, builds a deployable package of the code, builds a virtual machine image that the package is installed to, and then registers the virtual machine within the Netflix servers. At this point, the old build continues to run while a load balancer diverts traffic to the new build. The new build is monitored for a short time for errors so that should a problem occur, the load balancer can cut back to the previous good build. Therefore, Netflix has adopted continuous integration and taken it to its purest form. A developer can check in a change and, within the time frame of this build process, real customers will be using it! Continuous integration is a process all developers should be working toward; a robust testing suite is a firm foundation for enabling it. Clearly, this works for Netflix: Using a process that brings together different skill sets to deliver the common goal ensures Netflix is able to build and maintain a platform that handles more than 2 billion requests a day.

Automating (Nearly) Everything

Another huge advancement of recent times is the capability to automate nearly all your processes. Because Python is a scripting language that is simple to learn and flexible, it is easy to use Python to automate almost anything you need: testing, deployments, updating story management tools such as JIRA on a check-in, packaging of code, or even setting up a development machine for a new starter. How often do you rebuild and reimage your development machines? It is likely not very often, which can result in strange behavior due to variations in the version of the operating system installed, or even different versions of system libraries or dependencies being handled differently by different package managers. Writing a setup script in Python to create a perfect development environment for your development machines should not take long, and the time savings could be massive over the course of your project. For instance, you can re-create the perfect development environment with one command when someone new joins the team or if you need to rebuild your machine. Automating installation with a setup script in Python, means you can focus on code rather than battling with system administration.

This sentiment also goes for any other scenarios you can automate. You should look to automate any manual tasks you do on a regular basis. Just like you specified the default jobs for your paver build process that allowed you to execute `paver` to test and build your entire application easily, you can do the same for other tasks. For example you may need to process XML output, pretty-print format it and move it into the correct location in the file system. Why perform those same steps over and over when a one-line command can take care of it all? It also means that you have repeatable, stable scripts that handle all your major chores and tasks. Because it's likely everyone in the team will be making use of these scripts, any little defects or problems that occur within them are usually fixed by the developer who encounters them. When you use Python as the language for scripting, as well as your code, your entire team will understand and be comfortable making changes to or updating any scripts you write. If instead the scripts are in bash or another language that is not the main development language, you may find only experts in that domain will maintain the scripts. Using the whole team as testers of your scripts leads nicely into working in the public eye.

Working in Public

Another recent trend is that more and more companies are making their developers' code public and open sourced. All too often, code remains internal to the company or project it is being built for and is never exposed for the world to see and use. Sometimes perfectly legitimate reasons exist for this, such as security concerns, legalities (such as PCI compliance), or the need for intellectual property protection (in cases where your code is essentially your business and cannot be shared). However, in most other cases, what you have either written, as new or extended upon for libraries already in the public domain, would be valuable to the rest of the community. Share what you can!

Undertaking this relatively small step can bring huge advantages to the quality of your code while also improving the skills of your developers who are exposed to new ways of thinking and solving problems in code. By open-sourcing, you pool together the huge development communities that exist behind every language. Many developers are more than happy to give their time and effort in trying out software, providing patches and bug fixes, and suggesting improvements and new features.

Many tools make sharing and presenting your code to the open source simple; GitHub is a popular example. GitHub makes it easy for you to push your code to a public repository, together with short or extensive documentation. Developers can then look at the code, and download copies of it to their local machines—where they can work on it and then submit back "pull requests" to your GitHub page. These requests are essentially the changes other developers would like to make to your code; you can choose to bring them into the codebase or not, and discuss the ideas with the developer(s). It is an extremely powerful process that can bring excellent results, and many Python libraries have evolved from many developers working together to get those libraries to the stable, reliable state they are in now. Just take a look at the Requests library GitHub page (`https://github.com/kennethreitz/requests`) for an example of the community effort behind a key library.

One recent example of a company "working in public" is the *Financial Times* (FT) in the U.K. The FT has numerous websites across its entire web estate and found that many of them are fragmented and lack a common look and feel. Upon realizing this, the company's development community looked into a way to fix this and devised a way of standardizing every component that makes it onto an FT website. The community essentially set up a GitHub repository in which almost every single component was provided, with code, examples, and documentation around its usage, and put this out as public. This provided two key things. First, every developer at FT now has one place to go to find any element. Duplication of code is minimized because every developer can either take the element as it is or make suggestions for changes, which are approved or denied by the development community. Secondly, because the code is available in the public domain, developers have started to get help from the wider development communities while also providing a huge resource of well-written and documented code that other people can use and tweak for their own websites. FT receive help from the community in fixing any issues in their code, and in return they provide a huge learning resource on how to build software on the scale of a mainstream website like the FT.

Netflix is another example of working in public. As mentioned earlier, Netflix built up an entire custom platform that serves more than 2 billion requests a day and has grown to be one of the major players in the new market of streaming media. Netflix is looking to provide its entire code to the platform that supports such huge data to enable other projects and companies to grow using the technologies it has designed. You could forgive Netflix for wanting to protect such an investment in time and people-hours, but the company has chosen to give back to the community what it has built. For Netflix to consider such a move shows that they believe the process offers some great benefits in working this way. It is a clear challenge to the conventional wisdom governing how code and tests should be worked on and reviewed.

Collaborating on Step Definitions

A huge new area related to testing and working in the public is a movement to share and distribute step definitions for use in acceptance tests. With acceptance tests came a great opportunity to write exactly what functionality a given feature was supposed to deliver—and write it in simple language. However, this means that for every team around the world defining acceptance tests, there is a lot of duplication going on with many teams writing step definitions for how to visit a home page, or make a call to a service, or click a button or link, and so forth. It is sensible to follow the same ideas of crowd sourcing and collaboration used for code development code for step definitions. For example, sharing on GitHub pages gives access to a worldwide community to help in developing reliable, reusable step definitions.

Luckily, the community has acted upon this and the Cucumber website now offers a way to access collaborative step definitions. Cucumber Pro, shown in Figure 12-2 (`https:// cucumber.pro`), is the first step toward building a solution like this, but currently must be paid for. It is designed around sharing collaborative definitions across your team and the rest of your company but, you can easily envisage a service that allows for easy sharing of step definitions in a wider community, which results in the emergence of a standard set. A service like this would prove a huge help when starting a new project: It could provide you with a series of ready-made step definitions to quickly write your first feature files.

FIGURE 12-2: Cucumber Pro, the first step toward collaborative step definitions.

Final Thoughts

This book has introduced testing techniques and tools that are in mainstream use within the Python development communities. It set out to challenge the types of testing you may already do, and explain the benefits and impact of having a dedicated, comprehensive testing suite in place from day one of writing your code. You looked at everything from the makeup of your team to the development process using Agile methodologies and the various testing techniques of unit, acceptance, documentation, performance, and smoke testing. All these types of testing essentially add up to provide you with many layers of coverage across your application and confidence in what you are delivering to your customers. By building all the layers of testing into the actual process of development as opposed to an afterthought at the end of a project, you always have a safety net of checks being performed on what you have built. This means fewer bugs in production, happier customers, and well-rested developers (who hasn't been awakened by calls in the middle of the night if something crashes and burns!).

One of the key areas of testing that was introduced is acceptance testing—an area in testing that is certainly set to continue to see huge growth and adoption following its recent success. The ability to write tests in plain English (or the language of your choice!) is extremely powerful; it brings great clarity and facilitates collaboration across different skill sets and responsibilities within your teams. Everyone from Product Owners, Analysts, Developers, and QAs to DevOps can write and understand at least the feature files in acceptance tests. This means they can be shared and checked to see if they accurately articulate the business requirement that is to be expressed. You accumulate a huge amount of testable documentation around your application that expresses every feature it is capable of. It is advisable to keep checking in the development communities for advancements in the tools and techniques in acceptance testing; this is an area (especially in Python) that will continue to see huge growth and development because it helps to drive quality in applications alongside established practices such as unit testing.

Following the testing, you then looked at how to automate and streamline your testing and deployment mechanisms. By adopting continuous integration within your teams, every check-in of code is tested, packaged, and deployed to the environments where you need it. You remove many manual processes and ensure all your code goes through the same testing process. Continuous integration also facilitates great parallel working, ensuring that features are being tested together as they are *integrated* into the rest of the code so that you can detect, and fix any issues early.

Deployment was covered in-depth. You looked at the quickly evolving world of cloud platforms and how you can leverage them to greatly benefit your organization. Cloud deployments give you, as a business and software delivery team, the control and flexibility over the application and costs, as you need them. With so many options for going to the cloud, it is becoming hard to ignore and it is certainly worth following the advice in this book to try it out. You may discover that moving your code to the cloud is especially beneficial. All these techniques will help ensure you and your company can build solid and dependable software, which will be increasingly crucial as society becomes more reliant on computer systems.

Resources

Financial Times GitHub: `https://github.com/Financial-Times`

Netflix GitHub: `https://github.com/Netflix`

Netflix 100 Deployments a Day: `http://www.infoq.com/news/2013/06/netflix`

Example Python Stub Server: `https://github.com/tarttelin/Python-Stub-Server`

VCR.py: `https://github.com/kevin1024/vcrpy`

Requests Library GitHub: `https://github.com/kennethreitz/requests`

Cucumber Pro: `https://cucumber.pro`

Index